Artists' Voices
Calligraphy

The Amin Gulgee Gallery, 2006

D1737356

OXFORD

UNIVERSITY PRESS

OXFORD
UNIVERSITY PRESS

Great Clarendon Street, Oxford OX2 6DP

Oxford University Press is a department of the University of Oxford.
It furthers the University's objective of excellence in research, scholarship,
and education by publishing worldwide in

Oxford New York

Auckland Cape Town Dar es Salaam Hong Kong Karachi
Kuala Lumpur Madrid Melbourne Mexico City Nairobi
New Delhi Shanghai Taipei Toronto

with offices in

Argentina Austria Brazil Chile Czech Republic France Greece
Guatemala Hungary Italy Japan South Korea Poland Portugal
Singapore Switzerland Thailand Turkey Ukraine Vietnam

Oxford is a registered trade mark of Oxford University Press
in the UK and in certain other countries

ISBN-13: 978-0-19-547359-9
ISBN 10: 0-19-547359-0

Title image by Asad Rahman

Printed in Pakistan by
Mas Printers, Karachi.
Published by
Ameena Saiyid, Oxford University Press
No. 38, Sector 15, Korangi Industrial Area, PO Box 8214
Karachi-74900, Pakistan.

Calligraphy

Artists' Voices
Divine Text

Contents

Letters

Biodata

Calligraphy

Amin Gulgee Gallery
Dish Dhamaka, 2002

Gallery Introduction

The Amin Gulgee Gallery began in 2000 with an exhibition of Amin Gulgee's sculpture. The artist continues to display his work in the gallery, but he also sees the need to provide a space for large-scale and thematic exhibitions of both Pakistani and foreign artists. The Amin Gulgee Gallery is a space open to fresh ideas and different points of view.

The gallery's first such show, which took place in January 2001, represented the work created by 12 artists from Pakistan and 10 artists from abroad during a two-week workshop in Balochistan. The local artists came from all over Pakistan; the foreign artists came from countries as diverse as Nigeria, Holland, the US, China and Egypt. This was the inaugural show of Vasl, an artist-led initiative that is part of a network of workshops under the umbrella of the London-based Triangle Arts Trust.

The second show at the gallery, which took place in the spring of 2002, was entitled "Uraan" and was co-curated by Niilofur Farrukh and Saira Irshad. This was an exhibition of 100 paintings, ceramic pieces and sculptures by 33 national artists. A thoughtful survey of current trends in Pakistani art, the exhibit was originally intended to be displayed at a prominent gallery in New Delhi. However, the political climate between the two countries was such at the time that the show was unable to travel to India.

The gallery's third show was curated by Amin Gulgee. It took place in the winter of 2002 and was entitled "Dish Dhamaka." For this thematic show, 22 Karachi-based artists were asked to work upon a satellite dish, that ubiquitous symbol of information, entertainment, or unwelcome outside cultural values, depending on how the artist saw it. The fourth show at the gallery, which took place in December 2004, was of the Italian artist, Gino Marotta.

These two catalogues document the gallery's fifth and sixth shows. Co-curators Amin Gulgee and Sheherbano Hussain have asked artists from across Pakistan to create a piece for each exhibition. The first show is called "Artists' Voices: Calligraphy." The second show is called "Artists' Voices: Body."

We are extremely grateful to Ms. Ameena Saiyid, Managing Director of Oxford University Press Pakistan, for publishing the catalogues of these two exhibitions. We must also thank Ms. Ghousia Ghofran Ali, Managing Editor of OUP's Higher Education, Academic and Trade Division, as well as Ms. Batool Nasir, Design Manager at OUP. We wish also to thank Adnan Lotia for the clean layout that he created for the catalogues.

Finally, we wish to thank all of the artists and critics for their support and enthusiasm. Without them, these two exhibitions would not have been possible.

Curator's Statement

These two exhibitions happened in a very organic manner. Two years ago, Sheherbano Hussain approached me with the idea of curating a thematic show on the body. At that moment, I was busy with studio work, but I enjoyed the energy of this young graduate from the Indus Valley School of Art and Architecture in Karachi. We had another meeting and I told her of my interest in curating an exhibition on Islamic calligraphy. We then agreed that we would co-curate both shows, giving each other new ideas. We had a dynamic meeting with Ameena Saiyid, the Managing Director of Oxford University Press Pakistan, who offered to publish the documents for these two exhibitions.

Sheherbano and I set about the task of asking a cross-section of national artists, both young and established, to participate in the two shows. The art scene in my country is divided up into many camps and we asked artists from all points of view. Although the artist selection was diverse, most had never engaged with Islamic calligraphy. We insisted that the artists who kindly agreed to create work must participate in both shows.

Not only were they required to create one calligraphic work and one body work, but they were also asked to write statements for each show.

The aim of these two exhibitions is to learn about us at a moment in time. This is an artist family debate about two topics that have tremendous emotional resonance for us. The point was not to reach a consensus but to let the individuals speak for themselves. The hope behind these two shows is to capture these artists' voices.

Amin Gulgee

Curator's Statement

One of the dilemmas for artists in Pakistan today is the lack of platforms available to them to exhibit their work in a way that engages audiences beyond a certain level. While commercial galleries have played an important role in promoting and selling art, it is often left up to the artists themselves to take the initiative in generating an interest in art beyond its commercial and decorative potential. It is also no small feat to bring artists together and initiate a critical dialogue in an art community as disparate as ours.

While it is tempting to bemoan the current state of affairs, there are ways to work around it. For me, the first experience of such a collective effort was being on the curatorial committee of the Takhti Exhibition in 2001, when a diverse group of artists and art critics pooled their efforts to put together a massive show.

After that experience, I became interested in curating a thematic show on the body. My idea was to ask artists from different points of view to use both conventional and novel mediums to examine a subject that has particular significance for us. The question was: Where to show the work? The most obvious choice was the Amin Gulgee Gallery, which is both accessible and can accommodate large-scale exhibitions. What also appealed to me was Amin's honest and friendly nature, and the fact that his gallery is open to diverse points of view.

To my delight, not only did Amin agree to co-curate this exhibition, but also proposed that we co-curate a calligraphy show of artists who had never before worked with that art form. We then decided to do the shows back-to-back, and to approach the same artists to participate in each. So we asked our group of painters, sculptors, photographers and filmmakers to engage with both ideas. We were overwhelmed by the response of the participants, who managed to create exciting, evocative works in a very short span of time. The experience of organizing these two shows has been a testament to the immensity, as well as the diversity, of talent in the field of visual arts in our country.

Sheherbano Hussain

Calligraphy: an Attempt to Engage

Contrary to the view of some, Islamic calligraphy is not popular among the artists of Pakistan. Of course, some Pakistani artists have engaged with calligraphy in the past, most notably Sadequain and my father, Gulgee, who continues to work with Islamic calligraphy in his paintings. Presently, the art scene is eclectic and artists are experimenting with many different mediums and topical concerns. Islamic calligraphy, however, is rarely attempted, and is somewhat unfashionable. Most of the respected galleries rarely have calligraphic shows.

On the popular front, Islamic calligraphy appears everywhere. There are billboards with divine text and many private homes have verses from the Quran emblazoned on their outside walls. This is generally mass-produced work; respected calligraphers are rarely commissioned. This great love for text is not only religious. Secular poetry also appears inscribed on the sides of public buses and rickshaws and people's names often appear on cars and taxis, both in English and in Urdu.

For this exhibition, my co-curator, Sheherbano Hussain, and I asked artists from across Pakistan to engage with Islamic calligraphy. *Khatati*, or the art of writing calligraphy, takes a lifetime of training. The point was not to ask artists to become calligraphers overnight, but simply to engage with calligraphy on some level. Though representative of the Pakistani art scene as a whole, these artists, for the most part, had not used calligraphy in their work before. Two exceptions are Athar Tahir and myself. Mr. Tahir initiated the Pakistan Calligraph-artists' Guild in Lahore in 1997. The Guild is dedicated to the heritage of penmanship, calligraphy and Calligraph-art in all forms and languages.

The idea behind the show was not only to create a dialogue on the subject of calligraphy, but to bring fresh ideas and experimentation to an art form that very much belongs to us. The hope was that thinking artists would engage with and re-appropriate calligraphy. This was a learning experience for me and an odyssey.

Sheherbano and I approached plastic artists as well as filmmakers and photographers. As we visited artists' studios trying to convince the artists to engage, interesting topics were addressed. Some artists like Nagori, who was politically vocal in the 1980s under the regime of General Zia-ul-Haq, when calligraphy was promoted as an art form, politely refused, while others, like Lala Rukh, who was actively involved in the Women's Action Forum during the same period, accepted. Some artists expressed their reluctance to engage with Islamic calligraphy because they felt that it had become too commercial. Interestingly, Samira Raja, who co-owns and runs Canvas Gallery in Karachi, did not share this view. As she stated to me, "Though calligraphy should be considered an art form, it is not, due to its religious connotations, and thus most art collectors refrain from buying calligraphy."

Just as we had hoped, the work produced for this exhibition takes many different approaches, both in content and in medium. The work can be organized into three broad categories. The first includes artists

Amin Gulgee

who have actually used Islamic text. The second is artists who have simply used Urdu or Arabic letters in their work. And the third is artists who have used secular text.

There is a genre within Pakistani art of painters involving themselves with the body. Two such women artists are Meher Afroz and Nahid Raza, both of whom have been actively working since the 1970s. For this exhibition, they chose to use the word "Allah" in their paintings. Their intuitive approach and formulistic skill are evident in their works. Rather then attempting calligraphy in the classical tradition, both artists incorporated it into their own visual language. Tasaduq Sohail takes a similar approach. In the past, his work has addressed the body in a personal, mythological narrative. For the exhibition, he, too, painted the word "Allah," incorporating it into his style. Another artist who has simply used the word God is Tapu Javeri. Painting with acrylic, he uses tree forms to spell "Allah." The use of the word alone, without any additional text, perhaps illuminates these artists' desire for the essence.

Moeen Faruqi's work largely deals with urban narratives. In his paintings for this exhibition, he has used the phrase *Alhamdulillah*— "Praise be to God"—in the square Kufic script and there are references to Mondrian in his work. Moeen links the geometric nature of the script to color. *Alhamdulillah* is a phrase often used in the vernacular. Another common phrase, *Mashallah*—"Praise to God"—is used by the young artist Auj Khan in his painting. The approach is painterly and the text appears in a tumultuous seascape. In her work, Sheherbano Hussain takes a formalistic and narrative approach. Her divine text emerges mysteriously from sections of her canvas. Wajid Ali, a recent graduate from the Department of Visual Studies at Karachi University, created in 1998 by the sculptor Duriya Kazi, translates the entire chapter of the *Surah Rehman* into Urdu. In this chapter, the phrase "Which of the favors of God can one deny?" is repeated again and again. The chapter enumerates the many things that God has created. Wajid explained that he refrained from using Arabic for his piece out of fear

of misplacing any punctuation and he wanted to claim this joyous text in his own language. Another young artist, Seema Nusrat, who majored in sculpture at the Indus Valley School of Art and Architecture in Karachi, has tried to evoke the essence of the Qalma through color in her work. The text appears as a border in her miniature. Finally, Shah Murad Aliani has created a sound piece for the exhibition. This work incorporates sounds familiar in the Islamic world, including the call for prayer.

Another group of artists does not attempt to paint or draw Islamic calligraphy. Instead, they appropriate divine text from popular sources or comment about its use in the historical context. Adnan Lotia and Adnan Malik have documented the popular use of Islamic calligraphy in Karachi in their video. Aasim Akhtar photographs religious text appearing as graffiti on a wall. The New York-based artist Saeed Rehman captures the energy of the urban use of calligraphy in his digitally-manipulated photograph. David Alesworth appropriates the computer generated text *Al Muqit*—God the

Provider—from one of the numerous small books on the Ninety-Nine Names of Allah that are available in the market. Naazish Ata-ullah and Imran Qureshi's collaboration refers to how divine text has been used historically on clothing. In their installation, an invocation to Allah for protection is hand-embroidered on cotton.

In the second group of artists, in which I am included, Urdu and Arabic letters are used in the work, but they do not spell out words. The sculptor Roohi Ahmed has used the first letter in the Arabic alphabet, the *alif*. The use of the *alif* is interesting because it has served traditionally as a measuring unit for the specific Arabic script the calligrapher uses. In Farah Mehbub's image of a single mosque passageway taken from different angles, letters appear as shadows. This digitally-manipulated photograph perhaps addresses the many approaches towards the divine. In Afshar Malik's energized drawing, Arabic and Urdu letters pay homage to the act of writing and penmanship. His drawing is a celebration of both freedom and control. This joy in the

act of writing is also expressed in the work of Riffat Alvi, director of the V.M Gallery at the Rangoonwalla Centre in Karachi. In her painting, she has used letters to create the surface of her work. The Quetta-based artist Akram Dost Baloch takes a sculptural approach. He has inscribed letters upon a wooden structure whose shape is informed by traditional Balochi folk motifs. Lala Rukh's contemplative pieces, "Hieroglyphic III" and "Hieroglyphic IV," use abstract Urdu script. The placement of the luminescent letters on the horizon is evocative of the divine. And, finally, in Shamyl Khuhro's black-and-white photograph, letters of a manuscript are magnified by a reader's glasses. The manuscript, the *Shahnama of Mahmud of Ghaznavi*, written by the calligrapher Firdausi in approximately 1250 AD, is from the artist's family collection. The book is an example of how, in the past, respected calligraphers not only inscribed the Quran, but were commissioned by royalty to create secular manuscripts for themselves.

The third group of artists has used calligraphy but it is not from a

religious source and is secular. In Nurjehan Bilgrami's multimedia work, text appears in Urdu in a commentary on American culture. The execution of it leads one, at first glance, to believe that it might be religious. Naiza Khan's triptych on latex is composed of three Urdu words—"Ready," "Wait," and "Silence"—taken from a feminist play by Sheema Kermani. She used a calligrapher to create the words in reference to the tradition. The painter Shakil Saigol also uses Urdu text. He, however, renders the script in his own hand. In his work, the body of a woman is created by using the words of a poem by the legendary Pakistani poet, Faiz Ahmed Faiz. In his painting, Anwar Saeed uses secular text from historical astrological charts. Similarly, Adeela Suleman appropriates a chart from astrological treaties rendered in the Maghrabi style, one of the many scripts of Arabic. Babar Sheikh employs another script, the Dewani, to create three words in Urdu—"Past," "Present" and "Future"—for his video. Two Lahore-based artists, Mughees Riaz and Ali Azmat, have used unintelligible text to create painterly surfaces for their work. Finally, Shakil Siddiqui, a photorealist painter, has depicted an open manuscript, perhaps a ledger waiting to be written upon.

In conclusion, this show was an attempt to create awareness and dialogue about a great art historical tradition. Artists were not only required to engage with calligraphy, but to write a statement about their works as well. Just as we had hoped, the mediums, approaches and concerns were diverse. However, as I have outlined, three groups of artists did emerge: Those who engaged with divine text; those who used letters from the Urdu and Arabic scripts; and, finally, those who worked with secular text.

I am very grateful to the artists for agreeing to participate in this exhibition, even though, for so many of them, it meant working outside of their comfort zone. As a sculptor who has used Islamic calligraphy for some of my work, I felt that their energy and thought were much needed to remind us all that once a civilization existed.

Amin Gulgee, co-curator of this exhibition, is a sculptor based in Karachi. He received a BA in Art History and Economics from Yale University; his senior thesis on Mughal gardens won one of the Art History department prizes. In the fifteen years that the artist has been working, he has exhibited his work in Pakistan, the Middle East; the Far East, Europe and the United States. For four years in a row, he curated an annual exhibition of Pakistani artists at the Karachi Sheraton. He also curated "Dish Dhamaka" at the Amin Gulgee Gallery.

On Writing: Situating the Discourse on Calligraphy in Contemporary Pakistan

Fig. 1

Read! Thy Lord is the most Noble. Who taught by the pen, Who taught man what he did not know

(Quran, 96: 3).

Well done, O scribe, who with a flowing pen
draws letters, beautiful as Mani's art!
A skilled calligrapher, whose radiant eye has scattered musk upon a camphor-sheet!

Idraki Beglari[1]

The art of beautiful writing, or calligraphy, is among the most rich and complex forms of expression in Islamic societies. The importance given to the Quran, the holy book recording the word of God, is the primary basis for the attention given to the written word. According to Muslim tradition, the Quran was sequentially revealed to the prophet Muhammad (PBUH) by the angel Gabriel; the words were memorized and later inscribed by Muhammad's (PBUH) companions. The Quran, as revealed to the illiterate ('*ummi* prophet, is the unique and complex document of authority in Islam. Its reading and recitation is considered a form of worship that bestows *baraka* (blessing) on those who see and hear the sacred words. Qurans were also illuminated in gold and pigments of abstract and floral designs since as early as the 8th century, a tradition that compliments visually the beauty of the words. Although reverence of the Quran defines Islamic preoccupation with the written word, calligraphic expression is hardly limited to religious subject matter. Poetry adorns books, buildings and portable objects; scientific treatises as well as manuals on cooking are chosen as sites for adornment and illumination. In this brief essay, I would like to introduce a few examples of calligraphy that define their historical and social contexts. The intent is to set a foundation for the multiple and varied artistic responses collated in this catalogue.

The Arabic script, although varying according to regional and linguistic particularities, is the common foundation upon which the Islamic art of writing is based. The distinctive characters of the alphabet developed around the 7th century CE, but it was not until the turn of the 9th/10th century that the writing of Arabic was codified and standardized by the 'Abbasid vizier, Ibn Muqla (Fig. 1). The result was a selection of 14 calligraphic styles based on proportional systems of form and layout. Thus, the importance of a visual aesthetic was established early on in calligraphy, with treatises on further refinement and the appropriate function of the various styles. Among the most important factors in ornamental writing was composition, both of the words and of the manner in which they were to be situated on the page or on the object. The use of calligraphy ranged widely from beautifully inscribed and illuminated Qu'rans to include such diverse functions as unreadable monumental epigraphy and chancery documents stored in the imperial treasury.

Sites for the location of calligraphy are as varied as the meaning of the words themselves. One of the earliest and most powerful uses of monumental calligraphy (epigraphy in this case) is that designed for the Dome of the Rock (Bayt al-muqqadas) in Jerusalem (Fig. 2). Built in 691 CE to mark the occasion

Kishwar Rizvi

of the surrender of the city to the Muslim armies and as the earliest commemorative structure of Islam, the building is nonetheless an enigma.[2] A monumental octagon, with entrances on four sides, the Dome of the Rock is neither a mosque nor a burial chamber. The central space of the building is occupied by a large outcropping of rock, which acts as the focus of the entire ensemble. The clues to its significance can be found in the symbolism of the abstract designs, but more importantly, in its epigraphic program. The writing on the building covers the exterior cornices and continues on the interior, spiraling clockwise on the outside, anti-clockwise on the inside. Passages of the Quran were carefully selected to exhort the pilgrims and residents of Jerusalem to accept the new religion, while at the same time showing respect of the monotheist Christian and Jewish traditions that also called the city their own. The clearly written Kufic inscriptions, rendered in intricate mosaic tiles, are easily read, both from a distance and from up close. Their legibility complements the imperial

iconography that is also displayed on the interior surfaces of the Dome of the Rock.

Among the most beautiful "texts" are those written on a group of 11th century ceramic plates from the Eastern Islamic world. Calligraphic slipware was popularized when the Samanid dynasty, which ruled 819-1005 CE in Khorasan and Transoxiana, came to power and initiated the reinvention and transformation of the Persian language. Great epics such as the famed *Shahnama* (*Book of Kings*, 1010) of Firdawsi was written at this time followed by 12th-century Sufi texts of great poets such as Farid al-din Attar (*The Conference of the Birds*) and Nizami Ganjavi (*Khusraw and Shirin*). The literary renaissance was echoed in the production of high quality ceramics, inscribed with Arabic proverbs and blessings (fig. 3).[3] The sayings reflect, on the one hand, the function of the object, its role in the acts of giving and receiving, for example, of food or of gifting the object itself. On the other hand, they point to meanings embedded in the texts, which focus on the giving

and receiving of knowledge. In the literary environment in which these ceramic objects (mostly plates and bowls) were collected, *adab*, or education of a moral and intellectual nature, played a foremost role in defining social codes of behavior. The calligraphic ceramics were an essential part of the enactment of those codes, both imagined and real.

The performative nature of writing and the import given to calligraphic text is best exemplified by the arts of courtly connoisseurship. A page from a calligraphic exercise is a good example of the aesthetic value placed not only on the inscribed word, but on the act of writing itself (fig. 4). This page, collected in an album of painting and calligraphy from mid-15th century Herat, shows a page covered with the repeated Arabic phrase "blessings coalesce around the generous."[4] The first sentence, on the upper right, is signed by the master calligrapher, Ahmad al-Rumi, below which is the same phrase repeated in the hand of the Timurid prince, Baysunghur. Thus follow a series of repetitions, signed by various courtiers and

Fig. 4

artists of the court. The fragmentary exercise helps us reconstruct the *majlis* environment within which works of art, poetry, and calligraphy were created and judged. Princes, courtiers and craftsmen gathered together as connoisseurs and cognoscenti, establishing multiple discourses on the aesthetic valuation of the arts of writing and depiction.

Historically within the context of Islamic art, calligraphy was given preeminence and the calligrapher's art considered to be the greatest aesthetic expression. Not unlike the reciter of the Holy Quran, the talented calligrapher was believed to be endowed with a divinely-sanctioned skill, regardless of whether he wrote Qurans or chronicles. His personal virtue was reflected through his "hand" which was able to write words of beauty beautifully. But the calligrapher was not just an instrument enabling the calligraphy, but was himself considered an educated persona, a littérateur. Positioned higher than the painter by those who compiled the biographies of artists and craftsmen, the calligrapher was one

in possession of great knowledge and an innate ability to delight both the eye and the soul of the beholder. In fact, according to popular belief, the first calligrapher was the prophet Muhammad's (PBUH) cousin 'Ali bin Abi Talib, who is revered both as a caliph and a spiritual leader. Thus, although religious sentiment may be missing in the words written, the art of beautiful writing is seldom distanced from its esoteric roots.

The ornamented word in Islamic culture is both a talisman and an article of beauty; it is also the subject of artistic and political inquiry. Artists in Pakistan have used calligraphy as a form of self-identification and also as a means of exploring their modernist idioms within an Islamic tradition. For example, the artist Sadequain (d. 1987) collaborated with poets and illustrated their works in highly politicized visual and textual narratives (fig. 5). Coming from a family of calligraphers, he was well aware of the power of language, particularly in the period after Pakistan's foundation when the tensions between merging traditional

Islamic values with the ideals of the modern nation-state were first being explored. These complex and unresolved tensions mark artistic paradigms in contemporary Pakistan, as elsewhere in the Islamic world. The result is a confrontation between an increasing hybridity in the works of art through internationalism and the global art market, and a need to validate regional distinctiveness.

Calligraphy and miniature painting have emerged in the past two decades in Pakistan as two sides of a polarized debate on authenticity. The education of both the calligraphist and the miniaturist involves learning from earlier prototypes (sometimes taught by masters, or *ustads*) and to varying degrees familiarity with an arcane and romanticized art historical past. The idea of delving into the history of this art in this manner is in itself the product of a self-conscious search for an "authentic" Pakistani/Islamic art form. Just as attention to calligraphy in the 1980s was channeled through the patronage of the neo-Islamist government of General Zia ul-Haq, the current obsession with

Fig. 5

the miniature is arguably driven by Western (and westernized) perceptions of what Pakistani art should be. In both cases the expectations are forced through an Orientalist rhetoric that equates historicism with traditionalism. However, at stake in the art of the Islamic world, as exemplified in the current case of Pakistan, are neither the arts of writing nor those of depiction, but the nature of modernity itself. In capturing and critiquing their cultural heritage through calligraphy and the miniature, artists may thus enable themselves to finally own the history of Islamic art on their own terms; through their acts of repetition and reinterpretation, they initiate a discourse that deals cathartically with the multiple histories of colonial hegemony that have dominated much of modern art in the non-West. In so doing, these artists represent a transition of Islamic art into the future, one that is local and yet complexly polyvalent; one that is meaningful to them, but has relevance to modern art regardless of national boundaries.

1 Translated in A. Schimmel, *Calligraphy and Islamic Culture*, (New York: NYU), 1984.

2 Grabar, O., *The Shape of the Holy: Early Islamic Jerusalem*, (Princeton, N.J: Princeton University Press), 1996.

3 Pancarolu, O. *"Serving Wisdom: The contents of Samanid epigraphic pottery,"* *Studies in Islamic and Later Indian Art from the Arthur M. Sackler Museum, Harvard University Art Museum*, (Cambridge: Harvard University Press), 2002; pp. 58-68.

4 Roxburgh, D., *The Persian Album 1400-1600: From dispersal to collection*, (New Haven: Yale University Press), 2005.

Fig. 1. 'Abbasid Quran, 9th c.; Chester Beatty Library, Dublin.

Fig. 2. Detail from the Dome of the Rock, Jerusalem; photo courtesy of the Aga Khan Visual Archives.

Fig. 3. Samanid bowl, 9-10th c.; Arthur M. Sackler Museum, Gift of John Goelet, 1958.22 (pre-conservation image).

Fig. 4. Timurid calligraphic exercise attributed to Ahmad al-Rumi, Herat, before 1433; Topkapi Palace Museum, H2152 folio 31b.

Fig. 5. From *Paintings from Pakistan*, (Islamabad, Pakistan : Pakistan National Commission for Unesco), 1988.

Kishwar Rizvi teaches the history of Islamic art and architecture at Barnard College, Columbia University. Her primary research is on representations of religious and imperial authority in the art and architecture of Safavid Iran. She has also written on issues of gender, nationalism and religious identity in the contemporary art and architecture of Iran and Pakistan. She is finishing work on her book, *The Safavid Dynastic Shrine: Architecture, Piety and Power in 16th and 17th –century Iran*. She has recently edited, with Sandy Isenstadt, *Modernism and the Middle East: Politics of the Built Environment*, forthcoming.

Stories in Subversive Text

Arabic inspired calligraphy occupies a space between identity and politics in Pakistan and, in the last five decades, artistic intervention has transformed it from its classical orientation to a postmodern expression. As the artists' perception of calligraphy has changed from a symbol of identity to a component of a subversive strategy, its assimilation in visual arts continues to evolve.

In earlier decades, the authority of the written word and its meaning were central to the painterly interpretation of artists like Hanif Ramay and Shakir Ali. The scale and conventions of Islamic calligraphy that the artists had experienced in manuscripts and architecture impacted their easel paintings and murals. It is in these calligraphic works that they negotiated the idiomatic influences of modernism with the established framework of diverse scripts. The existing limitations of the ink palette was expanded by vibrant oil pigments, and tools like the brush and "knife" began to enrich the surface with textural treatments not seen before. Each artist carefully selected the script of his preference, if he did not invent one of his own, and a growing modern sensibility introduced new spatial configuration to these paintings of Quranic texts.

In Sadequain's works, calligraphy and forms are seamlessly entwined. He simultaneously looked at the classical format and innovated it while working with the unconventional shapes of roughly hewn marble slabs and hides. In the huge ceiling dedicated to Allama Iqbal's verse at the Lahore Museum, he arranged calligraphy in spheres of text that swirl through a nebulous path in the vast canopy of the inner roof.

With Gulgee, it has been a marriage of calligraphy and the gestural energy of Action Painting that marked a final departure from the conventions of the pen. This process brought a new spontaneity and open-endedness to what had been a rigidly articulated formulaic balance of forms. Amin Gulgee, his son, has inherited the same passion for the calligraphic form. As a sculptor who works in metal, Amin has had a long engagement with calligraphy that started with the symmetry and balance of the formal scripts and has led to a free juxtaposition of suspended and layered alphabets. With each new edge his work pushes to calligraphy, Amin discovers new possibilities within it.

Shemza, who moved to the UK in the 1950s, found calligraphy by default. In his article, "Recovering Cultural Metaphors," Rasheed Araeen informs that Shemza turned to calligraphic forms as an outcome of an identity crisis when his encounter with the dominant art discourse in his new homeland left him alienated. His interest lay in the underlying rhythm of the script. The abstract structure and pared down elements of the alphabet broke the template into an abstract pattern of color and forms. His "Roots" series was executed just before his death. According to his wife, it was painted when "Shemza felt a need at this time of his life to return to his own soil to nourish his roots." Zahoorul Akhlaq picked up the thread of conceptual engagement where Shemza left off. He did several works that concentrated on the negative spaces within calligraphy. These two artists discovered the

Niilofur Farrukh

deeper aesthetic resonance of the elaborate scripts.

The contemporary artist's interface with calligraphy has been with printed and digital text for promotion and marketing. Until recently, this printed text originated not from a mechanized process, but from the calligrapher's pen. Handwritten pages were etched on the printer's matrix, a practice still alive in the designing of logotypes and headlines of Urdu board sheets. With the increased outreach of Urdu typographic software, calligraphic skills were no longer necessary for the artists of the electronic era.

Handwritten or printed text, rather than grand statements in elaborate calligraphy, have increasingly found their way in contemporary art. From Arabic to Urdu, a language shift also began to take place as "casual calligraphy" echoed the egalitarian voice of wall chalking and graffiti in dissident art.

In a recent interview, Zarina Hashmi, the New York-based artist of South Asian origin, confessed that the Urdu title of her works, which have

often been interpreted as exotic elements in the West, were actually intended to foreground Urdu, a language threatened by a radical script change. In India, where the original script of Urdu, Nastaliq, is replaced by Devnagri, there is a genuine danger to the phonetic character and historical legacy of the language. She elaborated that the presence of Urdu, the language of the Muslims of South Asia, aims to make visible her religious and cultural identity at international exhibitions. An increasing number of artists in Pakistan have begun to sign their work in Urdu for similar reasons.

A message in elegant Urdu script proved a provocative act when Rasheed Araeen created a billboard design in the UK that praised the British for their racial tolerance. Its language and script, which were accessible only to people who were victims of racist violence in the South Asian enclaves, was successful in voicing a crucial issue in the public space.

In Imran Qureshi's Neo-Miniature paintings, the "vasli" surface of handmade paper is embedded with

yellowing pages from handwritten notes and do-it-yourself manuals. Loaded with connotations of colonial cultural intervention and sometime personal inscriptions, these fragments of history create a subtext to his social commentary.

The official patronage of Quranic calligraphy in the context of Zia ul-Haq's Islamization process of Pakistan may have been the turning point that weakened the link between creativity and the Arabic calligraphic tradition. Once perceived as the favored art of a dictator, some artists self-consciously de-linked from it and took up social activism. This period of official patronage for Quranic calligraphic paintings that had little to do with aesthetic excellence was one of interference in the freedom of expression and tested the allegiance of artists. For some artists, the nation's agenda of conscience prioritized citizens' rights and strengthened political and social identity through their work.

No longer driven by the idealism and optimism that Quranic calligraphies had symbolized with their link to the

glorious chapters of Islamic history
in the earlier years of Pakistan, the
contemporary artist is compelled to
deal with the reality of untold stories
of a people that can only be written in
"subversive text."

Niilofur Farrukh is a Karachi-based art critic, curator and art activist. She is the editor
of *Nukta: Art Journal from Pakistan* and is currently President of the Pakistan section
of the Paris-based International Art Critics Association (AICA). Her book, *Pioneering
Perspective*, focuses on the pioneering role of three women artists of Pakistan.

Calligraphy and Figure: a Dichotomy

The reaction to and status of Islamic calligraphy, at least within contemporary Pakistan, presents a definite indifference, if not a defiance to, this ancient art form. It is not linked with progressive thought or art, possibly because there has been a gradual shift towards a Western art education in our country, which is where current art discourse seems to be centered. The art of *khattati*, or calligraphy, by its very nature is an exercise in repetition. Western liberal arts education is, on the contrary, about discovery, change and a linear movement; progress is measured in terms of a linear change. Thus, this dichotomy between our past and our present puts us in a relationship of contradiction and confusion. Those who do create works based on calligraphy are not considered mainstream, although there have always been exceptions among artists.

The preference of Islamic text as an art form during the regime of Zia ul-Haq no doubt resulted in some artists having pushed their imagery to the extreme, in defiance of this link to authority. What seems very interesting, at the same time, is the parallel iconography on the street that reflects a far more intimate link to Islamic text. We see the Ninety-Nine Names of Allah displayed on billboards and at major arteries in the city. After the turbulent 1980s in Karachi, when ethnic violence was strife, the local government put up holy verses dealing with brotherhood and unity all over roundabouts. Underneath this official façade, however, there resides popular taste whose security, emotional and psychological nourishment is provided by religious verses.

Perhaps a more natural link to text is through the Urdu language, its script being the same as the Arabic and Persian. And maybe there is a need to widen the focus on calligraphy, which is seen only as religious text. Text, in the Kufic, Nastaliq or other scripts, has long been a part of the imagery that informs the artistic sensibility particular to this region. In Persian or Mughal miniatures, calligraphy has been integral to the manuscripts that were read like a book rather than put on the wall as a work of art in the modern sense. Among contemporary artists, Zarina Hashmi's compelling woodcuts and etchings have always integrated text, mostly in Urdu, with the visual. In her recent series of maps and boundaries, Urdu words such as *Baitul Muqaddas* (Jerusalem), *New York* and *Jenin* form part of the dialogue. Earlier work incorporated words like *deewaar* (wall), *chaukhat* (doorway), *chand* (moon) and *sooraj* (sun). Etched in her mother tongue, these words act as a reference to language as a vehicle of thought, memory and conditioning. Ghalib Baqar, the watercolorist, repeatedly refers to the poetry of Mirza Ghalib, Meer Taqi Meer and Zauq, merging Urdu/Persian text as a visual component with his imagery as he pushes the boundaries of this traditional medium into a more experimental arena.

Within the imagery that informs visual aesthetics outside the art gallery, text, or calligraphy as we may call it, is visible in street/local anecdotes painted on the "yellow devils" (local buses). These include phrases such as *Maa ki dua* (Mother's prayers), *Dekh magar piyar se* (Look, but with love), *Pappu yaar tang naa kar* (Friend Pappu, don't bother me!). The designer Maheen Khan uses this very theme as the source of inspiration for her

Amra Ali

recent Gulabo clothing collection. The iconography that the text feeds on is often of doe-eyed beauties, half-women and half-horse, flying over Karachi. Interestingly, though, floral imagery combined with *chamkpatti* (beaten silver tin decoration) and imaginary landscapes are predominant and recurring elements that suggest the choice of the artist in opting for nonfigurative, floral and design-based iconography. This approach may be based, firstly, on an intuitive impulse towards floral and geometric design-making in the region, and, secondly, on conditioning that we have received as children, when we were told that making the human form meant having to breathe life into it on the Day of Judgment. This concern must linger or reside somewhere in our psyche and affect our approach to art and image-making in relation to the figurative and the nonfigurative.

A prejudiced approach towards calligraphy today is part of a larger problem of an educational system that has failed to inform, educate and inspire its students of the past art forms of this area that could be carried into the future as significant forms of expression. Perhaps, first, we need to distance ourselves from the colonial mindset that continues to feed our own prejudices and promotes self-censorship. The understanding and relationship to calligraphy and of calligraphy to the figurative in art have somehow remained confined within the political context of the 1980s and of certain brief periods in our young history in a negative way. It must, however, be understood in the larger framework of its historical significance and the cultural baggage that it entails.

Amra Ali is an art critic based in Karachi. She is a founding member and senior editor of *Nukta: Art Journal from Pakistan*. She has contributed reviews and essays to major publications in Pakistan, as well as *Art India*, among other international publications. She is currently the Secretary of the Pakistan Section of the International Art Critics Association, and has been a Nieman Affiliate at Harvard University.

Musings on Calligraphy

Since the earliest days of mankind art has been an obvious phenomenon of the human race. In a simplified form, it is seen as craft or folk art practiced in village communities. It has always been present and always will be. Times change along with fashion, but as history tells us, art in its numerous forms withstands catastrophe, oppression and dictators. The declaration of "degenerate works of art" and the ensuing persecution of artists and burning of books in Nazi Germany during the 1930s resulted in New York becoming the center of contemporary art and artists and the source of Abstract Expressionism.

At an exhibition in Karachi a few years ago, the distinguished Chinese artist, Professor Liu Bio Shin, now held in high esteem in China, elaborated on how, during the Red Guard era in China, he was forbidden to paint. He was assigned to a forced labor camp where for ten years he worked as a farm laborer. He kept his art alive by scratching images in the dust with corn stalks late at night, then rubbing them out before discovery. Centuries

earlier, Chinese artists "spoke" to each other in a secret language of symbols to express their views on the forbidden topic of politics.

Such stringent oppression of the arts has never been practiced in Pakistan. A supreme indifference has been closer to the mark. Researching the era of General Zia-ul Haq, it appeared that calligraphy was never state-sponsored; no instructions were issued by that regime to allow the practice of any particular art. It is on record that on the eve of the opening of an exhibition of paintings by Sardar M. Arbab, held at the National Art Gallery in Islamabad, the General is quoted as saying: "Islam permits the practice of all arts may it be sculpture, painting, ceramics, singing, and music." Evidently not dancing, though, as the exquisite dancer, Nahid Siddiqui, was forced to leave the country to pursue her art after signing a paper declaring that she would not represent Pakistan by dancing abroad.

Artists such as Shemza and Hanif Ramay, who began working with

calligraphy in the 1950s, Shakir Ali and Naqsh, who had worked in calligraphy as an aesthetic exercise at times, and Sadequain were not concerned with popular movements or markets. In 1970, Gulgee created a stunning artwork for Expo 70 in Tokyo, using calligraphy on copper. In 1974, he assimilated the discipline into the masterful painting he made for the Islamic Summit held in Lahore. The move towards calligraphy by numerous lesser known lights during the Zia regime was in part inspired by admiration for the work of Sadequain and Gulgee, as well as coinciding with the market trends and expedience of the time. We are talking of the late 1970s and the 1980s here, the earliest days of an art market. In Karachi the public was flooded with exhibitions of so-called "calligraphy." The Arts Council showed little else. Unfortunately, artists without any background in the discipline created crude works that did quite well with buyers, who also knew little of the finer points of the art. These were usually hung in offices for transient visitors to admire. The most explosive

Marjorie Husain

reaction to this development in my experience was from the outspoken artist Bashir Mirza who, during the eleven years of the military regime, hung up his brushes and refused to show his work.

One must not forget the work today emerging from the Calligraph-Art Guild in Lahore, and the annual international exhibitions that take place, as well as beautiful work produced by skilled exponents of the art who continue to work individually.

Marjorie Husain was initially involved in art as a painter, but soon discovered the great need for documentation of art and artists in Pakistan. For the past two decades, she has committed herself entirely to writing on art. Her articles and reviews appear regularly in the country's leading newspapers and magazines. She is the author of four books, including the only text book for local art students in Pakistan, *Aspects of Art*, which is available both in English and in Urdu.

Q&A with Ismail Gulgee

Q: When did you become interested in Islamic calligraphy?

A: More than forty years ago, in the early 1960s. I was amazed that people from the desert could have evolved something as beautiful as Islamic calligraphy. This was a people who started with only the most rudimentary of scripts. Of course, for the first couple of hundred years, almost nothing happened with calligraphy. The Quran was still memorized, and passed on from generation to generation orally. There arose the need to not only write down the Quran, but to develop the script in which it was written. This was the divine word that was being written, after all. Those who developed calligraphy, gradually, over the generations, did so with hearts full of love. They saw a bird flying, or the way the wind shifts the dunes, and they began to imbue their calligraphy with these visual wonders.

Q: You are a self-taught artist, aren't you?

A: Yes. And I am also a self-taught calligrapher. I studied the masters of the past until I was able to write in any of their styles. There are rules, of course. But, after a certain point, there are no rules. Everything is intuitive. There is an order to calligraphy, just as there is an order to the universe. That order is truth. God has created the universe, the perfection of the universe, from the atom on. Through love and devotion, you become part of that order, that fabric, that structure. If you are an open and sensitive person, you reach a point where, if you see that something moves beautifully, then you know that it is working, just as the original calligraphers did. To do modern calligraphy, you have to understand its roots.

Q: Many of your contemporaries were influenced by Western art. Is that also the case with you?

A: If I have taken one thing from the West, it is the freedom of Action Painting. But I have tried to focus that freedom. I have tried to give it direction and meaning.

Q: You are also well known for your portraits in both lapis and oils. Has your calligraphic work influenced your other work?

A: Certainly the freedom that I have found within calligraphy has helped me with my other work. You can see this in my drawings especially, in the openness within them. I do these works very quickly. My hand moves faster than I could ever command it to. It's a wonder even to me. If there is love in your heart, the work comes naturally, no matter what it is you're doing. In my work, nothing is predetermined. I simply have a feeling in my heart that everything is going to work out.

Q: Most of our artists today are reluctant to take on calligraphy. Why is this so?

A: Islamic art is an orphan. It has no mother or father. While patrons like the Aga Khan have managed to revive an interest in Islamic architecture, no fresh perspectives have been offered to revive an interest in calligraphy. If you give support to our artists and calligraphers, more exciting work will be done. But there is no support. If Muslims don't care about their own art, why should anyone else? Look at all the Arab rulers, with their money and oil. They have done nothing. We don't even have a space to show our work in.

Q: Do you think there should be art in public spaces?

A: It is absolutely essential to have work in public spaces. The common man is so extraordinarily uncommon. He looks at things through his heart, which is the doorway to understanding.

Artists'

Voices

Divine Text

Untitled
18" x 18", acrylic on wood

When I was asked to do a calligraphic painting for this exhibition, I was moved and inspired and a bit apprehensive, because in order to do justice to calligraphy, one has to have a certain command over the basic skills of this discipline.

Meher Afroz

Untitled

I have always been inspired by calligraphic manuscripts and scripts and have used the same, extensively, in my paintings, most notably in my Amulet series. When I was asked to do a calligraphic painting for this exhibition, I was moved and inspired and a bit apprehensive, because in order to do justice to calligraphy, one has to have a certain command over the basic skills of this discipline. Since I was excited, I decided to work on it anyway, and after contemplating a few ideas and possibilities, I started to paint and experiment with Arabic letters. In my opinion, the letters of the Arabic alphabet have their own individuality and impact. I have explored the balance and the rhythm of the letters and how they join to make words, which in turn, have their own aesthetic appeal and power.

By writing Allah in the center of my painting, I have tried to show the universality of the Creator. I have depicted the entire universe as contained in one name: Allah.

G/94, Islamabad
11" x 15", color photograph

> "The writing on the wall or calligraphy is a model of freedom. For one thing, it calls our attention to art created from the purest motive: the desire for expression."

Aasim Akhtar

G/94, Islamabad

There was so much handwriting on the wall that even the wall fell down.

Christopher Morley

I must have driven three miles through Islamabad in search of a piece of "writing on the wall." What I saw was a city encircled by walls in their new vanilla-colored garb—pristine and immaculate. I missed the graffiti. It had been erased because it was feared it might incite religious fervor. I had always found the graffiti to communicate messages that were colorful, poetic, humorous, artistic, prophetic, loving, hopeful, frustrated—but rarely hateful. These are photographs of paintings of those words, and of words that paint pictures.

The writing on the wall—in this case, calligraphy—is a model of freedom. For one thing, it calls our attention to art created from the purest motive: the desire for expression. These artists know that their "creations" are likely to be painted over within a few days, so they are not out looking for immortality, or even a product that might be kept, admired, sold or envied. These are prayers and wails, and yet, paradoxically, they can be re-experienced as needed because they have been captured through the eyes of a camera.

Al Muqit
27" x 36", digital photographic print

> " What I have wanted to do with this work is to speak of the divine in terms of the everyday struggle to live, the small things we all do, the lists of things to achieve in any given day as a background to a prayer of hope and thanks. "

David Alesworth

Al Muqit

It has been an interesting journey I have taken in trying to arrive at a work that feels like my own and yet begins to address some notion of what this show is about. I have had to do my share of research, which has been wonderful, but it has not left me feeling any closer to a solution in the work; in fact, it has made it just so much more evident all the unintentional harm I might commit in my attempt to speak with another's text.

What I have wanted to do with this work is to speak of the divine in terms of the everyday struggle to live, the small things we all do, the lists of things to achieve in any given day as a background to a prayer of hope and thanks. I have chosen to work with *Al Muqit*, "The Nourisher", one of the Ninety-Nine Names and a prayed-for presence in the life of the householder. The text is not my own, but is overlaid on my daily lists of things to do: food to buy, tasks to achieve. My own handwriting is almost an equal mystery to me, although I can trace its evolution (or descent perhaps) from a script defined by a school fountain pen. The unfortunate outfall is that I often cannot read my own writing.

In this work, I wanted to create an impression of illumination, of calligraphy as divine light burning through the everyday. As an outsider and a mark-maker, I wanted to approach its boundaries, my marks rebuffed by some unseen force field, unable to achleve Union. I am not sure if I succeeded in saying these things, but that is what I meant by this.

پھر تم اپنے رب کی کس کس نعمت کا انکار کروگے
پھر تم اپنے رب کی کس کس نعمت کو جھٹلاؤ گے

> "Every time I read the Surah Rahman, I find new colors, new meanings and it seems that this ocean of blessings is expanding and keeps moving forward until it goes beyond the comprehension of a humble being like myself."

Wajid Ali

Untitled
66" x 16", ink on canvas

Untitled

Mujhe dhal de kissi shakal mein kay uchaal dey
Kaheen reh na jaey koi kar, meray kooza gar.

Calligraphy–regardless of its language, be it Urdu, Persian or Arabic—has its own built-in sense. Quranic script has been around for centuries; it keeps changing its form, color and place; in other words, it keeps adapting itself to conform to the current period of time. The Holy Quran has the depths of an ocean; the deeper you delve, the more you discover and every *ayat* is layered with multiple meanings. The Quran caters to every age.

I have translated the Surah Rahman, an ayat that glorifies the Creator and reminds us of His many blessings, which are difficult to deny. In this day and age, it seems we are failing in our duty to thank the Creator for His many blessings. Every time I read the Surah Rahman, I find new colors, new meanings and it seems that this ocean of blessings is expanding and keeps moving forward until it goes beyond the comprehension of a humble being like myself.

(translated from the Urdu by Sheherbano Hussain)

sound

> 66 My journey began with identifying the
> kufic style of calligraphy as the basis for
> my sound piece. I am attracted to its
> linear approach; the geometric balance
> which reflects nature as well as its Zen-
> like simplicity. 99

Shah Murad Aliani

Untitled

Being asked to produce a sound piece based on Islamic calligraphy is about as tough as it can get for me. Firstly, not having an expertise in, or passion for, either religion or calligraphy is daunting enough; combine that with somehow interpreting through sound "Islamic Calligraphy" and you will begin to appreciate the mountain that I have to climb. Nevertheless, I am happy that I have been asked to participate in this exhibition.

I am not aware of any such thing having been done before, so I will be boldly going where no man has gone before. Of course, I am aware of the various traditions available, like Sufi poetry, *hamds*, *naats*, *kaafis*, *qawalis*, etc., each of which pays audible homage to Islam. But this is an art exhibit. It is simply not enough to just mix various samples from, say, Sufi music to a backdrop of club trance beats and create a palatable piece, in vogue as that may be.

My journey began with identifying the Kufic style of calligraphy as the basis for my sound piece. I am attracted to its linear approach, the geometric balance which reflects nature, as well as its Zen-like simplicity. The goal is to somehow create that same feel through sound and also infuse a feeling of religious reverence and grandeur to the piece. Easier said than done, but, *inshallah*, I hope I have managed to do justice to the idea and created a piece that communicates what I have set out to do. If not, chalk it down to this being as abstract as religion is in this day and age, and make your own interpretation.

Above all else, have faith!

> " Our installation mocked the invasion from the skies over Afghanistan by the Americans who indiscriminately disbursed parcels of junk 'goodies' in yellow packaging. "

Naazish Ata-Ullah
& Imran Qureshi

Hasbun Allah
80" x 30", hand embroidery and drawing on cotton

Hasbun Allah

Hasbun Allah is the new title of a commissioned joint collaboration between Imran Qureshi and Naazish Ata-Ullah, which was undertaken for an exhibition at the Harris Museum in Preston, England. Our installation mocked the invasion from the skies over Afghanistan by the Americans, who indiscriminately disbursed parcels of junk "goodies" in yellow packaging.

This project is visited anew for this exhibition and the collaboration continues. The title of the work is an invocation to Allah for protection. History records soldiers going into battle with thin undershirts next to their skin under heavy armor on which verses from the Quran had been inscribed. Hence the cry for help, in this case, is both politically and spiritually relevant.

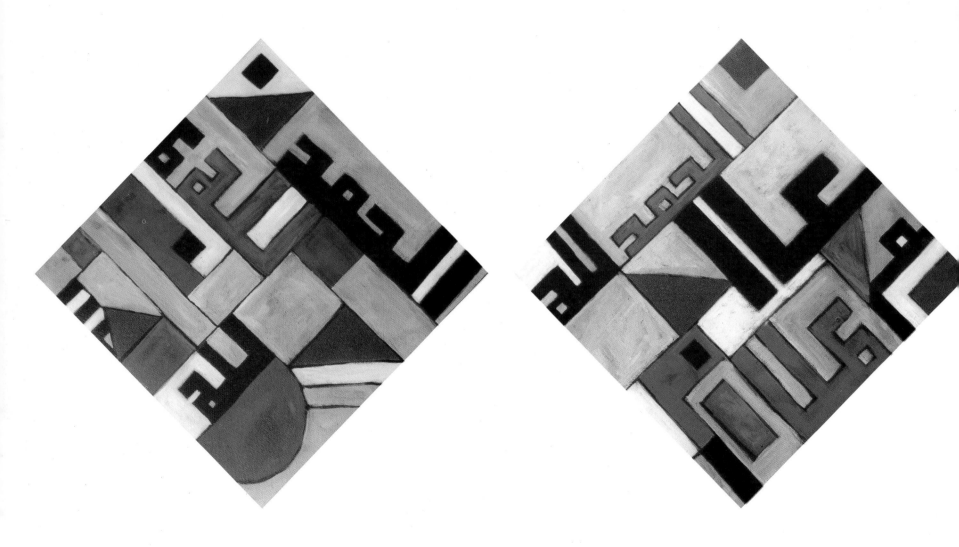

Kufic I, Kufic II
24" x 24", acrylic on canvas

" True calligraphy is a wondrous art form, learned and perfected over many years, and imbued with spirituality and mystery. It is the ultimate melding of text and image. Contemporary artists who use text in their work could learn so much from the form and shape of this art. "

Moeen Faruqi

Kufic I, Kufic II

While I have always been fascinated by calligraphy, I have also been averse to its commercialization in recent years. For this reason, I have long been hesitant to create works based on calligraphy. Too often we see calligraphy that is hastily done, or created solely to decorate homes. True calligraphy is a wondrous art form, learned and perfected over many years, and imbued with spirituality and mystery. It is the ultimate melding of text and image. Contemporary artists who use text in their work could learn so much from the form and shape of this art.

However, I looked upon this exercise as a challenge. I knew the curators well, and felt at one with their motives. The works submitted here are purely an experiment and exercise, an artistic diversion even. It does not attempt or claim to understand this sublime art form. It was simply an endeavor to briefly change course in my artistic leaning, an opportunity to experiment, to play with forms, and to learn something new.

I have also always been interested in geometric abstraction. I have often experimented with architectural forms, and the work here gave me a chance to join geometric forms with words from the Quran. The phrase *Alhamdulillah* is used as the basis for these works, where the words become a part of an abstract composition, I have referenced and drawn inspiration from the square Kufic script, so often beautifully used in the art historical past to create calligraphic square "mazes."

> " With the narrative tradition deeply embedded in my psyche, it became second nature for me to think in pictures and weave scenarios around anything or anyone who captured my imagination. "

Sheherbano Hussain

Ayat-e-Karima
36" x 48", oil on canvas

Ayat-e-Karima

Fantastic stories and haunting images shaped and nurtured my imagination as a child. An avid reader of fairy tales, I relished the sad and mystical tales of Hans Christen Anderson above anything else. My other source was my grandmother, who not only retained a vast repertoire of local fables and *djinn* stories, but also passed down heroic tales about prophets on impossible quests, ranging from Noah and Solomon, to Joseph and Moses.

Also, I grew up in a community where storytelling holds a very important place—every year, during the holy month of Muharrum, the tragic tale of the martyrdom of Imam Hussain, the grandson of the Prophet Mohammed (PBUH), in Karbala is narrated in Shia households and mosques the world over. Large processions are taken out to commemorate the martyrdom, offerings of food are handed out, and, in countries like Iran and Lebanon, the tragedy is even enacted on stage.

With the narrative tradition deeply embedded in my psyche, it became second nature for me to think in pictures and weave scenarios around anything or anyone who captured my imagination. This preoccupation with the enigmatic was to shape and direct the course of my artistic journey. Exposed mainly to Northern European art in my formative years, via my mother's collection of prints and reproductions, I was particularly drawn to the otherworldly images of the German romantic painter, Caspar Friedrich David. His painting titled, "Monk by the Sea," probably one of the first artworks I ever came across, profoundly influenced my way of seeing.

In an attempt to re-invoke that sense of wonder, I have appropriated "Monk by the Sea" in my painting, linking it up to the Ayat-e-Karima, a verse the Prophet Jonah (Yunus) is said to have recited inside the belly of a whale. I chose this verse because the Jonah archetype has always appealed to me; the concept of a reluctant messiah, fleeing from his own greatness, is one that most people can relate to.

The verse appears in sections in the painting, never as a whole, to reflect its elusive nature and also because it was recited in pitch darkness. The divisions of space, on the other hand, recall the zip paintings of the American painter, Barnett Newman, an artist whose work shares many qualities with Friedrich's sublime paintings.

> "God is seen through Nature, which in turn is appreciated through the Divine Book of Laws. The balance between the Laws of Nature and the Laws of God are made apparent by the symmetry within the work."

Tapu Javeri

Shajar
19" x 15", acrylic on board

Shajar

Photography captures a moment of truth. Art dissects that truth and makes it an illusion. My art is the crossroads between truth and illusion. Do not just look at it: look into it.

Though my medium has evolved from "painted photography," I have attempted to surpass that process and renew it into an art form with a more personal edge. The phrase "painted photography" can now be inverted and recoined "photo-painting" as the photo is now merely a secondary tool in my method. To this end, my technique of photo-art montage requires a delicate manipulation of photo collage onto board or canvas which I then overlay with paint. In the work that I have made for this exhibition, for example, the result is a dreamscape where the human form wrestles with emotion and nature. It is this balance between what is real (the photo) and what is surreal (the paint) that informs my work both visually and emotionally.

This particular painting is a radical change from my more figurative work. Entitled "Shajar," it seeks to convey an emotional response to the Divine. The spirituality that I present in many of my paintings is brought to the foreground in this piece. Here, Nature is a reflection of God's grace and artistry. Sinuous trees contort to form the word "Allah." They worship their maker, as do the birds suspended in flight and held up by the will of God alone.

In this piece, I have not used photography as a basis, but have tried to maintain a sense of experimentation. By affixing a Quran *rahael* to the center, I have

transformed a two-dimensional
acrylic-on-board painting onto a
three-dimensional plane. Thus,
the work must be visualized and
understood in its layered context.
God is seen through Nature, which
in turn is appreciated through the
Divine Book of Laws. The balance
between the Laws of Nature and the
Laws of God are made apparent by
the symmetry within the work. There
are no figures because man's self-
will necessitates disobedience; it
is Nature alone that upholds Divine
Decree without question.

Auj Khan

Mashallah
3" x 65", oil on canvas

Mashallah

Calligraphy is an exquisite sign and a weighty emblem of Muslim identity and faith. Within the heterogeneous mix of the contemporary world, shrunk and thrown together, this sign alludes to its people in much the same way that flags mark its nations. Besides being a marker in the broader context, it carries meaning of great reverence and importance as it embodies the sacred.

In our tradition of art, calligraphy has played a significant role and has served as a potent answer to creative solutions in our complex milieu of the secular and the religious. If art in churches marked the Christian spirit, calligraphy embellished interior and exterior surfaces of the Muslim space, be it a tomb or a mosque or a ceramic vase.

However, sadly, down the line, the linking of the calligraphic tradition to the national agenda in Pakistan and its use as an easy solution for the religiously contested act of image-making took the spirit out of the activity. In the history of Pakistani art, calligraphy now is much drained of its original meaning or meaningfulness as it now comes to function as a sign of a time and an attitude that was subject to hypocrisy and control. Perhaps it remains a bigger challenge now to release it from its past and reclaim and revitalize it in another manner?

For my part, I was interested in how the calligraphic and the venerated enter the vernacular. "Mashallah" has references to ones prized belongings, such as a new shiny house or car, or a sight of great splendor or attraction. Calligraphy is a discipline I am sadly unaware of, therefore there is much credibility in approaching it in line with my practice. As an artist today, I am interested in the Muslim experience and its essence rather than its ornamental aesthetic.

A cinematic sight of natural force refers to the essence of the ultimate and the mighty. The text and the sight of the image visusally construct the meanings it embodies.

Karachigraphy
video & sound, 8 min.

66 We used moving images and sound to capture not only the environment, but the experiential impact of these forms on the resident, the passer-by, the pedestrian, the motorist and the street-dweller. 99

Adnan Malik
& Adnan Lotia

Karachigraphy

Islamic calligraphy in Pakistan functions in three ways: it has the practical purpose of disseminating Arabic; it is the subject of academic and artistic exploration among traditionalists; and it is the vehicle for the popular, colorful and urban sentiment of a primarily Muslim nation. It is this third use of Islamic calligraphy that we have focused on.

The ubiquitous *mashallahs*, *allahu-akbars* and *bismillahs* that adorn public transportation, dwellings, commercial spaces and even public landmarks have their roots in religion, yet have now been appropriated to kitsch, iconic status. Devoid of their original meaning, they have been recontextualized into the Pakistani urban landscape as decorative cultural paraphernalia. Although social norms define and organize the presentation of these phrases, an amazing variation of form is observed in their adaptation to almost any medium imaginable.

Our process for documenting this use of Islamic calligraphy in Pakistan's urban capital involved moving through Karachi and observing the use of Islamic calligraphy in any number of public, commercial, and secular environments. We then sought out historical background on these forms, seeking to juxtapose their cultural roots with their current utilitarian or decorative functions.

Through dialogue with practiced professionals, academic masters and self-confessed novices, we formed an idea of public opinion crucial to our understanding of Islamic calligraphy within the multiethnic social pool of Karachi's citizenry today.

Lastly, we synthesized these elements, drawing upon our contemporary viewpoint as young, Westernized, irreverent and objective experimenters. We used moving images and sound to capture not only the environment, but the experiential impact of these forms on the resident, the passer-by, the pedestrian, the motorist and the street-dweller. The result is part-documentary, part-experimental video, a film that aims to record a cultural phenomenon as much as to rekindle interest and awareness in an omnipresent language of signs and symbols.

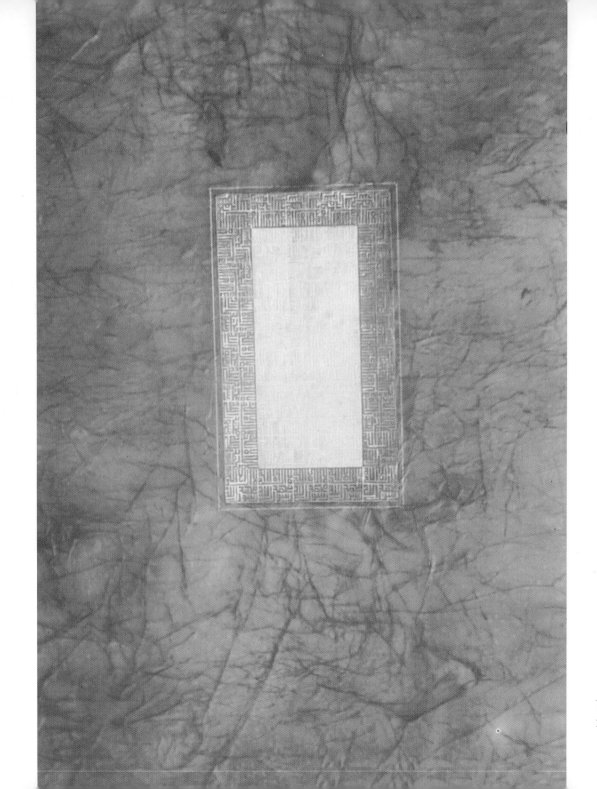

Untitled
17" x 24" gouache on wasli

66 I deliberately kept the phrase unrecognizable because I felt that it was more important to convey the meaning of the words as a visual whole than to depict the specific meanings of the words themselves. 99

Seema Nusrat

Untitled

Neither have I ventured into Islamic calligraphy before, nor do I have a vast understanding of the meaning of the Arabic script. Through my research into calligraphy, however, I was able to appreciate the ways in which calligraphy was explored through the ages in many regions. By looking at the various styles of calligraphy that have been practiced, I identified with the painterly treatment of so many of the scripts that I saw. In my personal opinion, I believe that calligraphy aims to express the spiritual meaning of the words through its techniques.

My piece explores calligraphy as pattern rather than the words themselves. The script I have used is *Kalma-e-Tayaba*, the first vow of any Muslim, a phrase that encompasses the entire spiritual being of all Muslims.

As an artist attempting calligraphy for the first time, I felt it vital that I understand the script I was using.

I deliberately kept the phrase unrecognizable because I felt that it was more important to convey the meaning of the words as a visual whole than to depict the specific meanings of the words themselves.

My primary concern as a painter is color, and, through color, I have attempted to portray my vision for the script. In this particular script, I envisioned luminosity.

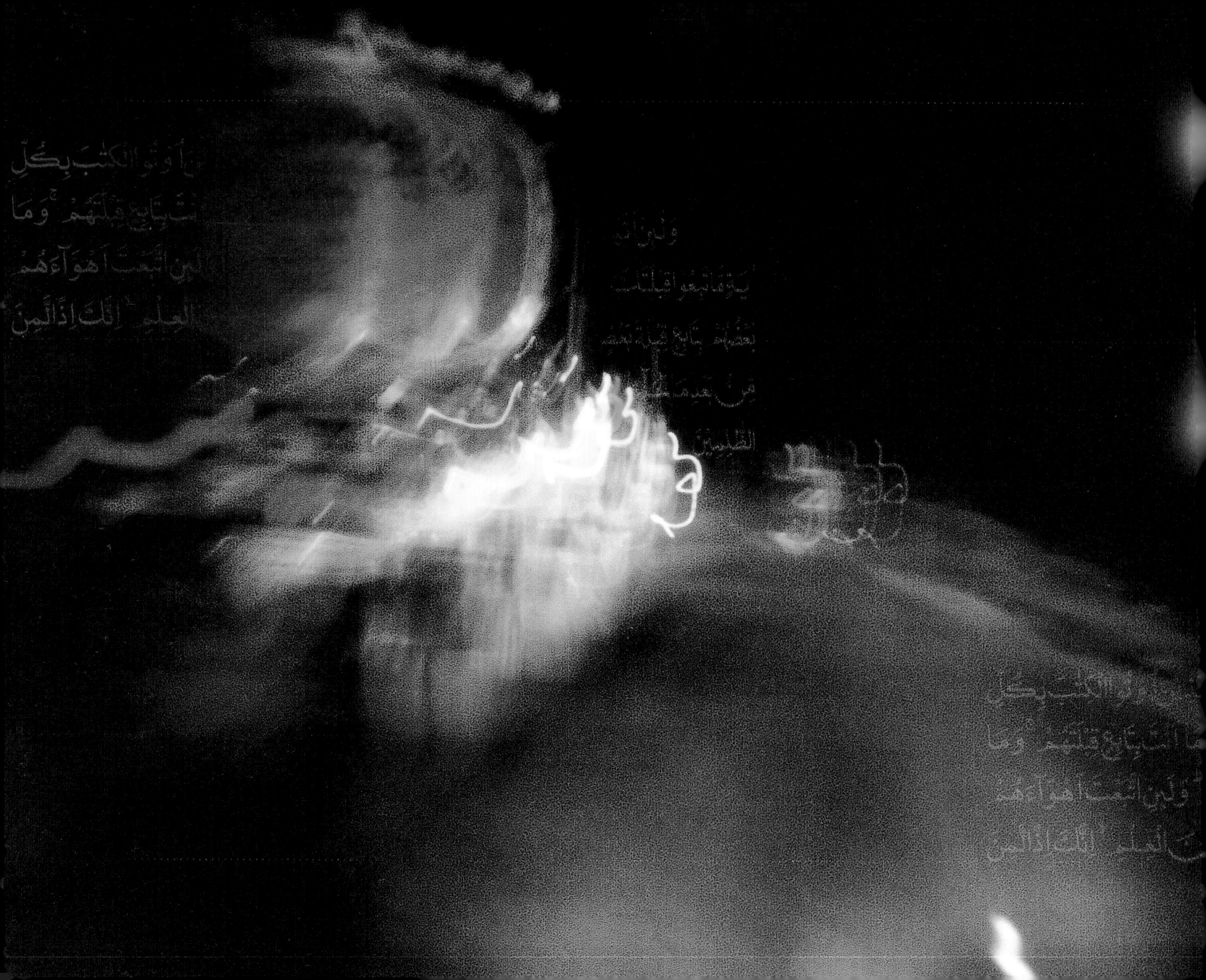

> " These pieces are about the connection
> between my life in Karachi as a young
> boy—the mixing of authority and religion
> in the form of the enforced *ayats* that I
> could never remember—and my time
> in Pakistan as an adult, when all my
> pleasure seemed to come from engaging
> in activities that were forbidden to me as
> a middle-class child. "

Saeed Rahman

Ayat-ul-Kursi
8" x 11", digitally manipulated photograph

Ayat-ul-Kursi

Growing up in Karachi in the 1970s and 1980s, I was enrolled at the Defense Authority Model School. I was marked at the school as holding the dubious honor of being "Roll Call # 1." By some strange fluke, I was the first student admitted. It was an army-run school that catered to mostly middle-class children, army brats and folks who lived in the Defense Housing Society. I was in the latter category. During General Zia's reign, among everything that felt queerly stagnant and regimented, the one thing that fluctuated was our school uniform. We would go back and forth from wearing shalwar kameez to shirts and pants. Eventually, this tug of war ended with a resolution: On Mondays through Wednesdays, we were to wear *awami* dress, while on Thursday and Friday, which were PT drill days, we were to wear—what else?—army clothing. (The girls, however, were to remain in shalwar kameez throughout the week, except that on PT drill days, they were ordered to wear blue shalwar kameez rather than white ones.)

The most memorable constant, however, was morning assembly. Every day for ten years, we would troop into the open air assembly area where one child was handpicked to recite an *ayat* as the rest of the students followed suit, raising their hands to proffer the *tarjuma*.

After the one child, picked among the hundreds of us, concluded his recitation of the *ayat* of his choosing, the rest would be asked about the meaning of the prayer. It became pretty routine. The *ayats* were familiar by now; there were three or four that were mostly picked and recited every day. I, however, found the entire experience frightening and would hide behind the other students to escape being picked for either recitation or translation. For even though most of the time the same texts would be recited, I could never get them right in my head. And, sure enough, when I was asked to perform the recitation in front of the entire assembly, just as I had imagined, in the middle of my recitation, the text escaped me. My mind just went blank. Somehow this mingling of authority and religion made my mind rebel in the strangest manner. It couldn't seem to remember lines and the order in which they were conveyed. To this day, I have not been able to learn most of these texts by rote. And the one or two I can remember, I recite at full speed without any pauses in case they escape me yet again. I engage in this exercise without any idea as to what I am saying.

I now live in the US and on my return to Pakistan after a hiatus of nine years, I insisted on riding public transport everywhere. As a boy in Karachi, I was never allowed on public transport (too lower class), and now it seemed all I wanted to do was ride buses. Sometimes, I would make excuses to go out just so I could ride on a bus yet again.

These pieces, then, are about the connection between my life in Karachi as a young boy—the mixing of authority and religion in the form of the ayat that I could never remember—and my time in Pakistan as an adult, when all my pleasure

seemed to come from engaging in activities that were forbidden to me as a middle-class child.

Allah

36" x 36", acrylic on canvas

> " It is not a bad thing to do calligraphy, if the artist takes a sincere interest in it. "

Nahid Raza

Allah

Art is about freedom. In the Zia period, calligraphy was promoted. Nobody can dictate to an artist what to do and what not to do.

During the Zia regime, I started my women series, even though it was difficult for me to take part in national exhibitions because of my nudes.

I never painted calligraphy and I never stopped doing figurative work. I continue to devote myself to it to this day.

Calligraphy is not my cup of tea. Yes, I can use calligraphic forms as an element in my work, as I have done in my painting for this exhibition. I used the name of Allah in an abstract manner.

It is not a bad thing to do calligraphy, if the artist takes a sincere interest in it. Even under Zia, many artists did calligraphy out of their own choice. I am thinking here of Gulgee, Jamil Naqsh, Hanif Ramey, Kamal and Mashkoor Raza. In countries

like Egypt, Turkey and Iran, a lot of very good work is being done in calligraphy. The Turks are especially fine calligraphers. When you use calligraphy in a creative manner, the way they have done, it is not only an admirable creative endeavor, but also creates value in art.

Untitled
8" x 10", oil on canvas

66 Too many of us think that calligraphy is only a commercial art, but that is not so. When we take something seriously, it is not commercial anymore. Serious artists should work in this medium so that we begin to explore new directions in this ancient art form. 99

Tasaduq Sohail

Untitled

When calligraphy became popular in Pakistan, I was in London, so I never tried it, and did not feel the need to do so. The other reason, obviously, is that my work is narrative and figurative. When I was asked to make something in calligraphy for this show, I thought it would be a good opportunity to try something that has always been around, but that I had never attempted before.

I think that artists should try everything before rejecting it. Too many of us think that calligraphy is only a commercial art, but that is not so. When we take something seriously, it is not commercial anymore. Serious artists should work in this medium so that we begin to explore new directions in this ancient art form.

Once I made the paintings for this show, I was happy with them, but felt I should continue along these lines, to see where else it might lead me. I am still working on calligraphic images, thinking about new ideas. I feel I should be able to produce some good work after a few months' work.

Al-Zahir (The Apparent)
7.5" x 10", mixed media with silver leaf
on wasli paper

> 66 The fundamental spiritual impulse manifests in colors that go beyond theory and have to be read, and felt, as symbols of state of being. The manner of paint application and attention to detail are prompted by the miniature technique. 99

Athar Tahir

Al-Zahir (the Apparent)

Traditional calligraphy celebrates skill. It is controlled and judged by rules set by past masters. Any departure from these rules is disdained, dismissed. Conformity is stressed. In short, every *aleph* must be the same.

Calligraph-art, a vibrant new genre, evolved simultaneously in Muslim societies across the world during the middle of the twentieth century. It is a major, original contribution by Muslims to the contemporary international art scene. Western aesthetics, social values and culture prompted Muslims to re-examine their priorities, heritage and conventional mind-set. Artists, not calligraphers, began to transform the roles and rules of calligraphy. This search parallels a Sufi's quest to go beyond the apparent (the *zahir*) to the inner (the *batin*), beyond form to the essence. Here meaning and form become one. Each calligraph-artist creates his own rules for a separate recognizable image. Creativity is stressed. In short, every aleph must be different.

This work is inspired by Sufism, informed by symbolic use of color and indebted to the rich repertoire of Mughal miniatures.

The fundamental spiritual impulse manifests itself in colors that go beyond theory and have to be read, and felt, as symbols of a state of being. The manner of paint application and attention to detail are prompted by the miniature technique.

As in any creative endeavor, the search for options and variations adds to a comprehensive understanding of the subject. Many letters of the Arabic-Persian-Urdu scripts have the added advantage of having three shapes: the initial, the median, and the final. These, when combined to form words, spawn a spectrum of limitless possibilities. Each letter-shape obliges one to engage with the many moods of the line. Each work so rendered teases one into thought.

Letters

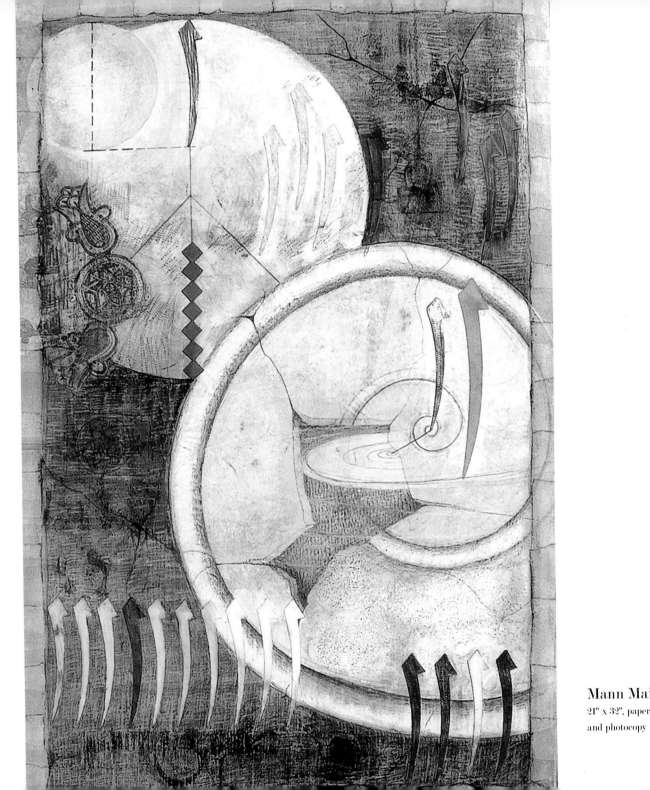

Mann Mai Alif
21" x 32", paper, copper foil, wax, pigment
and photocopy

" In the great Sufi tradition, one who is smitten by the love of God empties his heart of all but Him; the Alif of Allah pierces the heart and leaves no room for anything else. "

Roohi Ahmed

Mann Mai Alif

Oh! Friend now quit thy learning;
One Alif is all thou dost need.

Baba Bulleh

Revisiting the very first letter I learned to read and write as a child, ALIF, I was taken aback by surprise! The surge of energy that emanated from it completely engulfed me and brought back to mind the very first sensation of being able to identify, communicate and connect.

The feeling of joy and the sense of accomplishment at being able to read and write this single letter (as if I had mastered every possible thing within my young world!) slowly and gradually became mislaid as I moved on to the next letters—not to mention the mere complexities and distractions of growing up. Obliged to go back to the letters so that I could produce an artwork at this grown-up stage of my life, I started to approach calligraphy with a "no big deal" attitude, but was brusquely halted at the very first letter: ALIF. Yes, I was taken aback. It totally riveted me by its presence and I could not find the will or the desire to move on to the next letters, let alone venture into the realm of words or text.

Alif, alif, alif...I began to look again at its form and its geometry, its pivotal position within the realm of calligraphy, and also within Sufism. I was awestruck by the majesty of its presence and its comprehensiveness. The Alif (a line), created from a point (zero, nothingness), ventures forth in an endless variety of forms and rhythms. It radiates the origin of The One hidden within His manifestations. In the numerous styles of Arabic calligraphy, the Alif is a constant and is literally used as the diameter of an imaginary circle within which all Arabic letters can be written, again reflecting the **Primordial Act of the Divine Pen.**

Thy Lord is the Most Bounteous,
Who Teacheth by the pen,
Teacheth man that which he knows not.

(Surah al-Alaq, 96:3-5)

I felt myself repeating it incessantly, like *zikr*, **trying to unravel the depth of meaning encoded within its existence. I started making alifs on different surfaces with different mediums, like someone possessed. They were all around me; the spiral of their visual echo encircling me, and drawing me within. Glimpses of something elemental, like bright sparks of energy, emanated from it. I felt a sensation of something ubiquitous, elemental, and indefinable—and yet quite known and all-embracing! Alif, alif alif, mixed with flashes of memory...Alif—***aam, alif—***angoor**, alif—***anaar**, alif—***ammi, abba***...Alif—Allah!**

In the great Sufi tradition, one who is smitten by the Love of God empties his heart of all but Him; the Alif of Allah pierces the heart and leaves no room for anything else. Therefore, one need only "know" this single letter in order to know all that is to be known. As Hafiz proclaims,

There is no trace upon the tablet of my heart save the
Alif of the stature of the Friend.

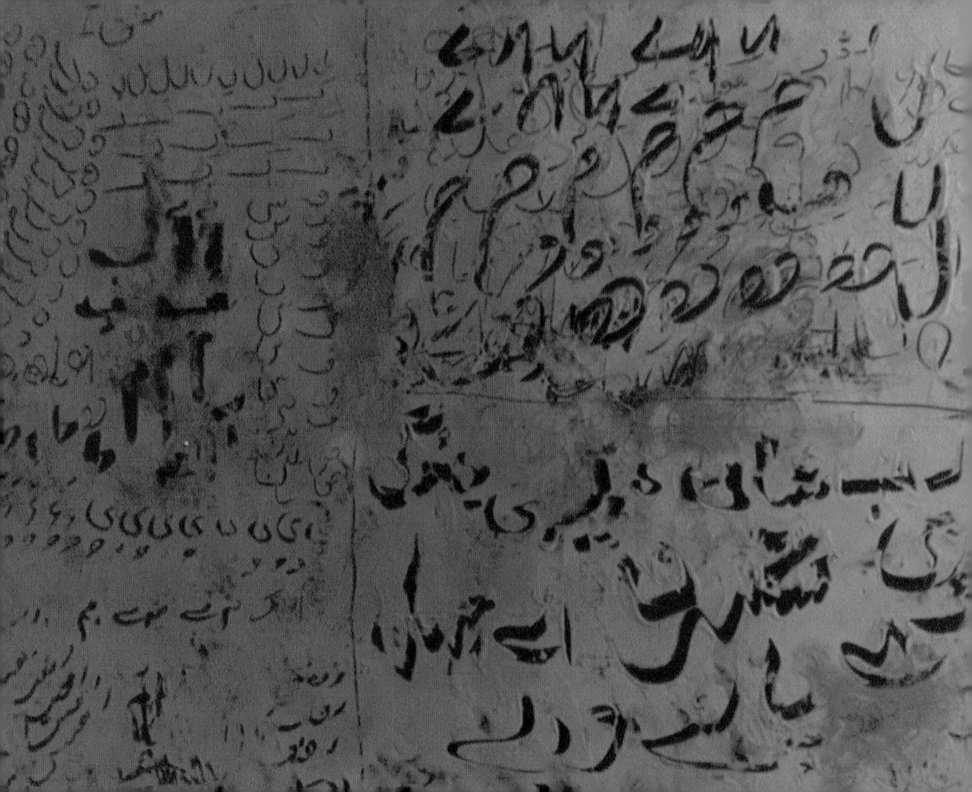

" I have been inspired by the rhythmical traits of music and dance so often apparent in the most inspiring examples of calligraphy. "

Riffat Alvi

Mashq
24" x 36", earth and acrylic on board

Mashq

The written word is considered the noblest and most distinctive form of Islamic art because of its association with the Quran. Beautiful calligraphic writings abound in Islamic art.

In my own work, I have been inspired by the rhythmical traits of music and dance so often apparent in the most inspiring examples of calligraphy. My approach is a non-disciplined one. Letters are spread across the entire space or canvas in a simple, spontaneous yet rhythmic manner.

Untitled
48" x 18" x 18", wood carving

> By enclosing a tablet within four pillars and arches, I have attempted to pay homage to Islamic architecture.

Akram Dost Baloch

Untitled

I see this sculpture as an addition to my on-going series of works in wood. I am pleased with its combination of curves, straight lines and geometry. By enclosing a tablet within four pillars and arches, I have attempted to pay homage to Islamic architecture. The engraved irregular "calligraphy" on the tablet suggests the character of Islamic or Arabic text without actually having an explicit textual meaning.

As in so much of my work, I have also included traditional motifs from my native Balochistan. In this composition, I have refashioned these traditional motifs in an attempt to create an aesthetic balance between the primitive and the modern.

Link IV: Stitches
90" x 18" x 16", copper and brass

> The word for welding in Urdu can literally be translated as 'stitches.' In this work, I have attempted to sew together my ongoing conversation with God.

Amin Gulgee

Link IV: Stitches

My paternal grandfather was a preacher. He used to walk every evening to his place of worship. One day he died there after saying his prayers. I was very young at the time, and I remember not feeling terribly sad because I did not know this reticent man very well. My cousin, Miko, and I were hanging out around my grandparents' house that day, happily ignored by our extended family. I can still remember the smell of *biryani* cooking in the large metal pot that sunny afternoon when my cousin turned to me and said, "Let's go and get some chili chips and a Coke." We both walked away from the funeral, content in each other's company.

My upbringing was non-ritualistic. We were never forced to pray. Although my parents are both deeply spiritual, they never imposed religion upon us. My father is a famous painter and, in his tremendously prolific body of work, he has used Islamic calligraphy. He has studied the calligraphic masters of the past and is able to write in any style he chooses.

There was never any pressure on me to follow in my father's footsteps. In fact, it was actively discouraged. My mother always told me, "Son, do not be an artist." I studied Economics at Yale University and I did a second major in Art History. It was then that I became fascinated by Islamic art history and my thesis was on Islamic gardens.

A good deal of my work as a sculptor has involved Islamic calligraphy. I have never claimed to be a *khatat*. Rather, I use one line from the Quran in one particular script of Arabic and repeat it over the years. To stay within these parameters is challenging for me. I also enjoy the idea of repetition and engaging with form.

In "Link IV," I have used the line from the Iqra *ayat*, "God taught humankind what it did not know." Again, I have used this line in this particular script over the years for my sculpture. This particular line was readable in my previous sculpture and yet in my Link series it no longer is. In "Link IV," the line is repeated six times and, although I have uséd every letter from the line, it can no longer be read.

A significant number of Muslims do not read Arabic. They learn to recognize religious text rather then read it. Having worked with this same line over the years, and having become so familiar with the shapes of its letters, they began to intuitively link together in my mind. The word for welding in Urdu can literally be translated as "stitches." In this work, I have attempted to sew together my ongoing conversation with God.

> 66 From a technical standpoint, calligraphy has scientific origins, with much focus on design, precise measurement and geometric patterns. 99

Shamyl Khuhro

Untitled
14" x 16", photograph

Untitled

The development of Islamic calligraphy is contemporaneous with the revelation of Islam in the 7th century AD as well as the development of the Arabic language, script and art form. While Islam was originally passed down to generations orally, the art of handwritten Arabic scripts of the Holy Quran developed rapidly and helped to spread the word.

From a technical standpoint, calligraphy has scientific origins, with much focus on design, precise measurement and geometric pattern. Yet there is an equal emphasis on soulful expressions of fluidity of lines and richness in color. Masters of this art form have attempted to balance these ideas to create a wealth of styles. Today these styles are known throughout the world of Islam, the differences in method being particular to various regions of the world.

My contribution to this exhibition is really a nostalgic one. While rummaging through my family library, I stumbled upon an old Persian manuscript with beautifully adorned pages that had always fascinated me. The central and most active part of the picture is the zooming of the camera lens into the seemingly dancing letters through the prism of the reader's spectacles. I felt the contrast of letters as seen closely and, at the same time, from a distance created an interesting effect. The reader is anonymous and incidental; his spectacles are used simply as a tool.

Ten Layers, Hidden Meaning
20" x 60", Fujiflex Crystal Archive color print pa[

> So renowned were Ottoman calligraphers, in fact, that a popular saying was that 'The Quran was revealed in Mecca, recited in Egypt, and written in Istanbul.'

Farah Mahbub

Ten Layers, Hidden Meaning

The architectural image prepared for this show was inspired from one of my favorite books, *The Secret of Secrets*. I incorporated Arabic letters, rather than sections or complete *ayat* from the Quran, because I felt the need to emphasize what I read earlier: How little we really know or understand the divine revelations. These letters for me were like a beginning without a conclusion.

Calligraphy means "beautiful writing." During the Middle Ages, Muslims cherished calligraphy as the premier art form because the Quran was written in Arabic and it represented the word of God.

Calligraphy came to decorate mosques and holy books. Writing was not only an artistic expression; it was a religious expression as well. I am not aware of present day practices, but in earlier times calligraphy was thought of as an expression of man's spiritual state: The purer the writing, the purer the heart. Therefore, the calligrapher had to be in *wadu* (ablution) not only to pray, but also when he touched the Holy Quran for the commencement of his work, be it for documentation or art.

Calligraphy has an exceptional place in Islam because it is strongly entwined with the Quranic revelation in two ways. At the outset, God's word in the form of the Quran embodies a sole confirmation of divine revelation, which was conveyed to the Prophet Muhammad (PBUH), but was then documented in script by his companions and circulated. Secondly, this revelation is described in the Quran as a "gracefully proportioned script," which is preserved with God on "pristine sheets of paper," and which is "beautiful" and "unsurpassable."

The history of Arabic calligraphy is interesting in all its various stages of progression. The one time that I can think of when that progression came to an unnatural halt was in Turkey in 1923 when President Mustafa Kamal Ata'turk abolished Arabic calligraphy. Despite this, modern Turkish masters are still considered to be among the leading practitioners of Arabic calligraphy in the Islamic world. This is not surprising when one recalls that, from the late Middle Ages onward, Ottoman masters were arguably the finest exponents of all the calligraphic scripts devised by the Arabs, the Persians and the Turks themselves. So renowned were Ottoman calligraphers, in fact, that a popular saying was that "The Quran was revealed in Mecca, recited in Egypt, and written in Istanbul."

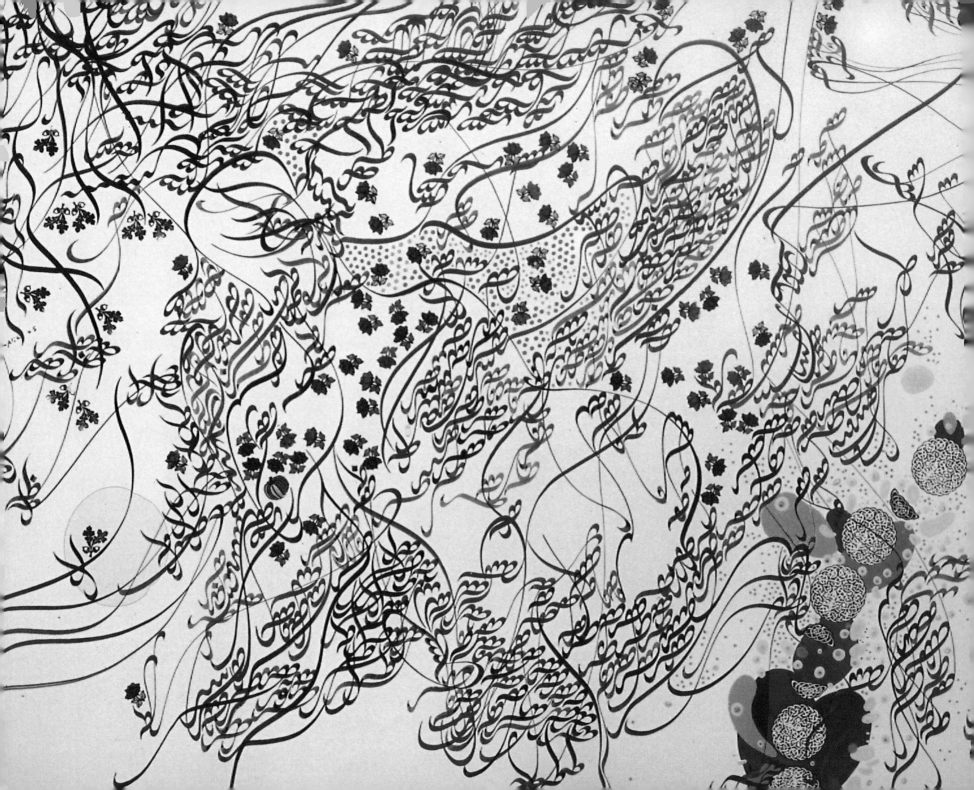

One wishes to have a non-ending flow of ink in the calli-nib on a sky-sized paper.

Afshar Malik

Fish Swim Clockwise in Their
Sea-Blue Cloud
9" x 28", mixed media

Fish Swim Clockwise in Their Sea-Blue Cloud

There is nothing wrong with flying in the air and drinking the cloud around you, nothing wrong with enjoying hundreds of dips between the ink and the calli-nib while a man elevates his body into the air. The motive is a humming of a desired tune. One wishes to have a non-ending flow of ink in the calli-nib on a sky-sized paper since the sky is limitless, singing is free and wine, the tastiest.

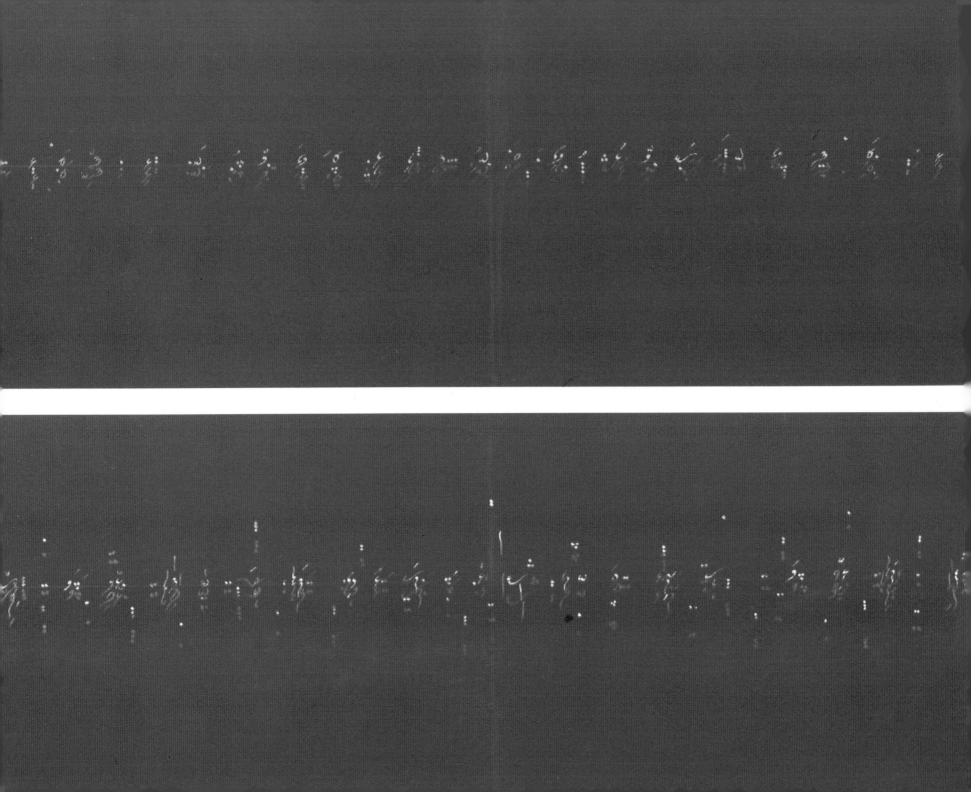

> 66 Calligraphy inspired me for its pictorial value, because it is like drawing. It is the most exacting drawing I have ever attempted, and the most abstract. 99

Lala Rukh

Hieroglyphics III & Heiroglyphics IV
24" x 8", silver paint and graphite
on carbon paper

Heiroglyphics III & Heiroglyphics IV

The *nukta* is to calligraphy what point is to line.

Beyond all the hype for and against Islamic calligraphy, the much maligned, much adored art, lies the reality of a highly sophisticated art form. What is little known about its history and evolution is the fact that the rules and principles of calligraphy were arrived at through a collective process and consensus among the most accomplished practitioners of calligraphy of the time. And what is more incredible is that the art of calligraphy emerged from the desert in a society that largely relied on oral traditions.

It has been a source of inspiration for generations of artists, from the most conventional to the most avant garde. While some may have knowledge of its rules, most are simply inspired by it. They have used it in a hundred different variations and combinations, techniques and styles.

Imagine! A tool determines the size, proportion, form and embellishments of an image. It is the most abstract of pictures, where the unit—the *nukta*—that the tool (*qalam*) describes becomes the basis of intricate mathematical configurations, marking time and space. One needs to sit with an *ustad* in order to truly understand the complexities of this unique art, and to see how within a strict discipline the qalam in the hand of the ustad can take one on a breathless journey into the realms of imagination. Perhaps it is this that has inspired so many generations of artists, or perhaps it is the division of time echoing musical divisions, or perhaps it is the striving for perfection achieved by rigorous *riyaz*, where the difference of a hair's breadth can create imbalance and disharmony. Whatever it is that has inspired them, artists have employed various aspects of it, in a hundred different ways.

Calligraphy inspired me for its pictorial value, because it is like drawing. It is the most exacting drawing I have ever attempted, and the most abstract.

''Hieroglyphics III'' and ''Hieroglyphics IV'' are linked to an earlier series of drawings that were also related to the ocean and calligraphic form.

Text

Quatrain
36" x 42", oil on canvas

> In my painting, those unspoken words that are not to be uttered are very keenly felt.

Ali Azmat

Quatrain

I have invariably used the human figure, almost exclusively in its anonymity or its universality. My paintings as a whole are human archetypes, recreating the story of humanity in potent images rather than words. In them, the collective soul remembers its own history.

The most positive aspect of my work is that it invites reflection and introspection. Moreover, the formal elements of my work, such as the combination of light, form, space, perspective and colors also engage viewers.

Expressing reactions to life through paint is the experience that merges art and life. I have always been interested in working with the human form, since it has been my major source of inspiration. My paintings are dominated by the human body and I use space to emphasize the solitude of the model. On the surface, my work is about arranging the figure in a rhythm. The women in my paintings have been idealized in pensive, submissive poses, characteristically reclining, to reflect their social context.

But above all, my fascination with the landscape of the human form and the solitary existence of my figures, reveals more about my state of mind than the person depicted. In my painting, those unspoken words that are not to be uttered are very keenly felt.

> Free the minds
>
> Free the words
>
> Free the letters

Noorjehan Bilgrami

Kiyoon na Amriki Saqafat ko Nazar Andaaz Kiya Jaey?
35" x 10", paper, acrylic, olive oil and acacia
Arabica gum on wood

Kiyoon na Amriki Saqafat ko Nazar Andaaz Kiya Jaey?

Till when should we remain in bondage….

Why should we be enslaved….?

Free the minds

Free the words

Free the letters

The Structure

The Grid

The Outer

The Inner

Unchain

Separate….

The Flight

Weightless

The Void…

Weightlessness…

Enough justifications -

Why should we justify?

Mine

Yours…

Ours…

N O W ….

nukhta… zer… zabar…..pesh…..

Tayyar, Intezar, Khamosh
48" x 16," paint and latex on wood

> **❝** Where do we place text and calligraphy in the work of artists? And how do we avoid a misinterpretation of image and text, where the visual is not subordinate to the literary? **❞**

Naiza Khan

Tayyar, Intezar, Khamosh

The contextual framework of these two shows has set into motion many thoughts and crossovers between two seemingly opposing notions— Quranic texts and the body.

My impulsive reaction to this brief was to integrate the two ideas. I felt they were inextricably linked, like two sides of the same coin.

I am interested in the calligraphy of sacred texts in terms of their meaning and interpretation and impact on our life. The idea of sacred texts from the Holy Quran and the use or un-use of the figure has many possibilities. The printed text embodies its own qualities as object and carrier of verbal information. There is a sense of freedom in using words as a material resource to work with and transform, making them autonomous, as much as the ink or stitching alongside them.

A lot of questions were raised that made me want to use words. Where do we place text and calligraphy in the work of artists? And how do we avoid a misinterpretation of image and text, where the visual is not subordinate to the literary? I wanted to place the viewer in a space between viewing and reading, where they were confronted with the same questions.

In this work, I want to use the idea of word as object that is perhaps not legible, but conveys sound or lack of it. It embodies this quality in a visual sense and a physical sense. So the skin of latex offers varying connotations, where words are visible and then submerged, the boundaries between them fluid and unstable.

Calligraphy with Clay Pot
30" x 24", oil on canvas

> 66 Every evening, I found myself striving to analyze the many color tones I saw in the sky. It was a private world without another soul in sight and only the sound of birds chattering in the trees. I wanted to transfer this vision to my own canvases. 99

Mughees Riaz

Calligraphy with Clay Pot

During my final years as a student, I began to explore the phenomenon of dusk. Early evening is a time when the sky over the river Ravi is a melting canvas of the palest shades of pink, blue and lilac.

My work is closest in style to that of the Romantics. The luminescent light of the sky was especially inspiring for me. Every evening, I found myself striving to analyze the many color tones I saw in the sky. It was a private world without another soul in sight and only the sound of birds chattering in the trees. I wanted to transfer this vision to my own canvases.

The large landscapes of the Punjab continue to inspire me and fill me with a sense of awe. Buffalos and crows often appear in my paintings. I admire the crow for his single-mindedness and stubborn disposition. The buffalo I admire because he is the great provider in rural Punjab. Whether directly or indirectly, my canvases draw their inspiration from the landscapes of my youth.

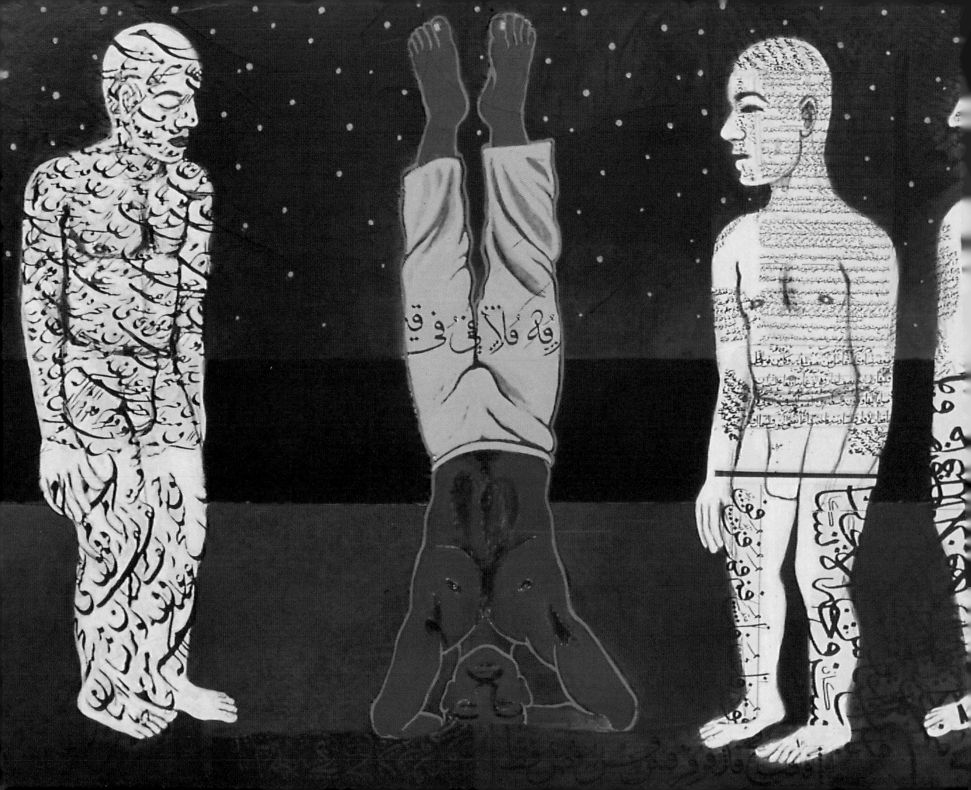

> Sometimes one feels like standing on one's head—a sad man, looking at the world upside down.

Anwar Saeed

Untitled
29" x 18", mixed media

Untitled

The social structure of this part of
the world is not based on human
nature and its needs. Instead, it is
based on feudal values of honor,
shame and guilt. That is why
sometimes one feels like standing
on one's head—a sad man, looking
at the world upside down. This might
actually be the other way around,
but the world around us is full of
pressures. It is a world burdened
with hollow sacredness of ideas,
concepts and language.

> " I have always been inspired by the works of great masters of calligraphy. I have always admired the flow of lines and the balance of design of this traditional Islamic art. "

Shakeel Siddiqui

Untitled
18" x 24", oil on canvas

Untitled

I have always been inspired by the
works of great masters of calligraphy.
I have always admired the flow of
lines and the balance of design of
this traditional Islamic art.

> The calligrapher's personal and subjective interpretation of the written word or verse is unique. It is this 'animated' aspect of the illustrated letter which fascinates me.

Shakil Saigol

Faiz's 'Raat Yun Dil Main Teri Yaad'
41" x 25.5", water color, gouache
and back ink on paper

Faiz's 'Raat Yun Dil Main Teri Yaad'

Calligraphy in its essence imbues the written word with a rhythm which resonates phonetically with an "inner rhythm." The calligrapher creates images which become animated with his vision. The calligrapher's personal and subjective interpretation of the written word or verse is unique. It is this "animated" aspect of the illustrated letter which fascinates me. Not being a calligraphist, my response is to render the written word in figurative form; in fact, the human form.

The Arabic alphabet is extremely pictographic and lends itself so elegantly to the artist's conceit.

For instance the *ain* represents the eye, *jeem* represents the camel. The arabesques are so flexible and so versatile rendered in stone, mosaic, on paper and in ceramic. They are immortalized in countless artifacts, in manuscripts and embellishing incredible monuments.

I, personally, lack the requisite command over the classical Arabic of the Quran. To me the sacred word of the holy book is for veneration, to be revered but not to be used for experimentation in case I inadvertently misrepresent a Quranic verse merely to create a design. I am essentially a figurative artist and not too comfortable out of my own genre.

Hence my choice of Calligraphy in Urdu. The verse I chose to depict is one of Faiz Sahib's poems. I don't know if it is a tribute befitting his genius. Traditionally, calligraphy in Islamic arts has employed freely the illustration of birds, flowers and animals, so I thought my attempt at Calligraphy had to be within my own framework. As I thought of how to give a form to the verses, it became an almost involuntary extension of my preoccupation with textiles and Jamavar shawls. The "design element" in the shawl was overtaken by the *takhallus* of the poet, while the poet's verses became the figure of his muse—each feature, each limb a fragment of the verse and the complete figure illustrating the eight lines in Nastaleeq. The complete lines are reproduced below the figure in Kufic script.

All forms of art are the artist's self-expression. They are also chronicles of the artist's life and times, a time capsule if you like. How relevant the artist's creation is, is for the viewer to determine, an act at once subjective and objective.

> " Just as the title of the work suggests, the installation revolves around the simple belief of fate and its related happenings, very much present in our society. "

Babar Sheikh

Taqdeer Toh Likh Dee Gaee Hai
video work

Taqdeer Tau Likh Dee Gaee Hai

Just as the title of the work suggests, my film revolves around the simple belief in fate in our society. The use of a monkey illustrates the frustration and helplessness of the everyday man.

Urdu calligraphy in a classical style appears and vanishes from time to time upon the palm of the hand. Even though the words used are fairly simple—such as "past," "present" and "future"—they appear to have a sacred overtone to them, only because of the use of the typeface.

**Whether Acute, Obtuse or
Naturally Right-Angled**
40" x 36", screen printing and acrylic

> Every text within it carries the desire to imagine who would read it. Whether the text is secular or sacred it pre-supposes and pre-determines its reader.

Adeela Suleman

Whether Acute, Obtuse or Naturally Right-Angled

Every text carries within it the desire to imagine who might read it. Whether the text is secular or sacred, it pre-supposes and pre-determines its reader. Thus, Islamic calligraphy also sets the rules. Even the most basic characteristic of the actual practice of calligraphy, which is taken for granted by non-practicing onlookers, requires a high degree of expertise. It is very important to know the placement of the letters on the surface because a page of calligraphy at once invokes a sensation of movement and rhythm.

This work examines the geometric interplay of Arabic letters to reflect the mindset of the artist working within the socio-cultural, political and economic context of General Zia's regime.

Meher Afroz
Roohi Ahmed
Aasim Akhtar
David Alesworth
Wajid Ali
Shah Murad Aliani
Riffat Alvi
Naazish Ata-Ullah
Ali Azmat
Akram Dost Baloch
Noorjehan Bilgrami
Moeen Faruqi
Amin Gulgee
Sheherbano Hussain
Tapu Javeri
Auj Khan
Naiza Khan
Shamyl Khuhro
Adnan Lotia
Farah Mahbub
Adnan Malik
Afshar Malik
Seema Nusrat
Saeed Rahman

Biodata

Nahid Raza
Mughees Riaz
Lala Rukh
Anwar Saeed
Shakil Saigol
Babar Sheikh
Shakeel Siddiqui
Tasaduq Sohail
Adeela Suleman
Athar Tahir

MEHER AFROZ

EDUCATION
1971   Bachelor of Fine Arts with honors, Government College of Arts and Crafts, Lucknow, India

SELECTED SOLO EXHIBITIONS
2005   Chawkandi Art, Karachi, Pindaar series
2004   Nomad Gallery, Islamabad, Replacing Realities series
2001   Chawkandi Art, Karachi, Zindaan series
2000   Wakefield Art Mill Gallery, Yorkshire, UK, Fragile series
2000   Bretton Hall Gallery, University of Leeds, UK, Fragile series
1999   Chawkandi Art, Karachi, Hisaar series
1999   Mount Castle Gallery, Columbo, Sri Lanka, Apparition series
1997   Chawkandi Art, Karachi, Niche series
1996   LRBT Show, Karachi, Hisaar series
1994   Chawkandi Art, Karachi
1992   Private Shows, Dubai & Abu Dhabi
1990   Gallery Interior, Islamabad, Portrait series
1990   Chawkandi Art, Karachi, Portrait series
1987   Chawkandi Art, Karachi, Mask and Puppet series
1984   Rohtas Gallery, Islamabad, Silent Voices series
1974   Karachi Arts Council, Karachi, Evolution of Symbols series

SELECTED INTERNATIONAL & REGIONAL EXHIBITIONS
2005   Beyond Borders, Mumbai, India
2003   Inspirations from the Indus, Hong Kong
2003   Laal Exhibition Art Gallery of Mississauga, Canada
2002   Baghdad Third International Festival of Plastic Art, Baghdad, Iraq
2000   International Exhibition, Sharjah, UAE
2000   Pakistan Another Vision, Brunei Gallery, London, UK
1999   PNCA group show, Amman, Jordan
1998   Printmakers of Pakistan 1947–97, Cartwright Hall, Bradford, UK
1996   Group show, Avignon, France
1995   Intelligent Rebellion, Cartwright Hall, Bradford, UK
1993   6th Annual Biennale of Dhaka, Dhaka, Bangladesh
1986   Pasadena Museum of Art, California, USA
1986   SAARC Countries Art Show, India
1986   Asia Exhibition, Dhaka, Bangladesh
1986   Women painters of Pakistan Show, Honolulu, Hawaii
1986   International Exhibition Triennale, Delhi, India
1978, 76 Western pacific Print Biennale, Melbourne, Australia
1974   Asia Today, Milan, Italy and other parts of Europe
1971   All India Fine Arts Graphics Exhibition, Calcutta, India

1970   Annual Exhibition, UP State Lalit Kala Academy, Lucknow, India

SELECTED GROUP EXHIBITIONS IN PAKISTAN
2002   Uraan, Gulgee Museum, Karachi
1999   Two Person Show, The Art Gallery, Islamabad
1997   Show on Karachi Carnage, Goethe Institut, Karachi
1996   National Show, PNCA Gallery, Islamabad
1995   PNCA & Alliance Francaise group show
1994   National Art Exhibition, PNCA, Islamabad
1993   Group Show on Violence, Goethe Institut, Lahore
1992   Women Artists Show, American Center, Karachi
1992   Print Show, American Center, Karachi
1990   Group show, Ziggurat Gallery, Karachi
1989   Women Painters of Pakistan, Islamabad
1989   Fourteen Painters of Pakistan, Indus Gallery, Karachi
1974   Women painters Show, PNCA
1973   6th Anniversary Exhibition, Contemporary Art Gallery, Rawalpindi
1972   National Exhibiton of Paintings, Graphics and Sculpture, PNCA

AWARDS
1996   Awards in painting at National Exhibiton, PNCA
1993   Honorable mention, 6th Annual Biennale, Dhaka, Bangladesh
1991   Selected for USIS International Visitors Program
1986   Painting selected for printing by UNICEF
1985, 77 1st prize in Graphics, National Exhibition, Pakistan
1982, 81 2nd prize in Graphics, National Exhibiton, Pakistan

WORKSHOPS & SEMINARS
1997   Servile Muse seminar, Goethe Institut, Karachi
1996   Workshop in Toulouse, France
1995   Painter workshop, Alliance Francaise, Islamabad
1993   Presented a paper, 6th Asian biennale, Dhaka, Bangladesh
1993   Painter workshop on the theme of Violence, Goethe Institut, Karachi
1992   Printmaking workshop with Walter Crump, American Center, Karachi
1991   Workshop on woodcut techniques, Kala Institute, San Francisco, USA

TEACHING EXPERIENCE
1990– Senior faculty, Department of Fine Arts, Indus Valley School of Art & Architecture, Karachi
2000, 03 Painting workshop, Women University, Rawalpindi
1999   Printmaking workshop, Fatima Jinnah University, Rawalpindi
1975–90 Fine Arts lecturer, Central Institute of Arts & Crafts, Karachi

1988   Printmaking workshop, Artists Association of Sind, Karachi

ROOHI AHMED

QUALIFICATION:
1999   Advanced Drawing Course, SVA, New York
1992   Dip. F.A., Karachi School of Art
1986   B.Sc., Islamia Science College, Karachi

EXPERIENCE:
- Imparting Art education since 1992 at Indus Valley School of Art & Architecture/ University of Karachi/ other institutes
- Contributed towards set and costume design for theatr plays
- Traveled nationally and internationally
- Worked on a number of commissioned projects
- Illustrated a few books

CURRENT OCCUPATION:
2005   Coordinator, Foundation Studies Program at the Indus Valley School of Art & Architecture
1992   Teaching the Foundation studies and sculpture
2002   Member of Vasl Art Trust (Under the umbrella of Triangle Arts Trust, UK)

WORKSHOPS/RESIDENCIES ATTENDED:
2003   "Vasl" – International Artists' Residency, Karachi, Pakistan.
2003   "Britto" - International Artists' Workshop, Valluka, Bangladesh.
2001   "Vasl" – International Artists' Workshop, Gaddani, Pakistan.
2000   A 3-month long residency to work with a theatre group and travel in Germany.
1998   Set Design Workshop conducted by Steffani Oberhoff from Germany, Karachi.
1998   Workshop on Sculpture conducted by Sandra Cros from Australia, IVSAA, Karachi.
1997   Set Design Workshop conducted by Syed Jamil Ahmed from Bangladesh, Karachi.
1996   Workshop on Restoration of Art works conducted by Mari Yamaryo from Japan, IVSAA, Karachi.
1994   Marbling Techniques Workshop conducted by Hikmut Barutcugil from Turkey, IVSAA, Karachi.
1992   Printmaking Workshop conducted by Walter Crump from U.S.A. American Center, Karachi.

SELECTED SHOWS:
2005   Street Art Inspirits, Harbourfront Centre, Toronto, Canada.
2005   Beyond borders, NGMA Mumbai, India.
2004   11th Asian Art Biennale, Shilpakala Academy

Dhaka, Bangladesh.

3   Vasl (work produced during the residency), The V.M. Art Gallery, Karachi.
3   8th National Exhibition of the Visual Arts, Al-Hamra, Lahore.
3   Group show, Canvas gallery, Karachi.
3   Britto work produced during the workshop, Dhaka, Bangladesh.
2   Dish Dhamaka, The Amin Gulgee Gallery, Karachi.
2   Aar Paar-2, An exchange between artists of Pakistan and India, exhibited simultaneously in Karachi & Mumbai
2   Roll Call, Group Show, V.M. Art Gallery, Karachi.
2   KARA-ART 2002, Group Show, SG Forum Art Gallery, Alliance Francaise, Karachi.
1   Group Show, Chowkhandi Gallery, Karachi
1   KARA-ART 2001, Group Show, SG Forum Art Gallery, Alliance Francaise, Karachi.
1   Takhti Exhibition – 2001, Gallerie Sadequain, Karachi.
1   Vasl (work produced during this workshop), The Amin Gulgee Gallery, Karachi.
0   KARA-ART 2000, Group Show, SG Forum Art Gallery, Alliance Francaise, Karachi.
0   The Experimental Space, Arts Council, Karachi.
0   Aar Par or Beyond Borders, an exchange between artists from India & Pakistan, exhibited simultaneously in Karachi & Mumbai
0   Pakistan: Another Vision – 50 years of painting and sculpture from Pakistan, presented by the Asia House and Arts & the Islamic World. A traveling show exhibited at various galleries in England
9   Citiscapes, Gallerie Sadequain, Karachi
7   Group show, Rohtas Gallery, Islamabad
6   Group Show, British Council Art Gallery, Karachi
6   7th National Exhibition of Visual Arts, National Art Gallery, Islamabad
5   Kanagawa International Print Exhibition, Kanagawa Kenmin Gallery, Kanagawa, Japan
4   Art Caravan, a mobile exhibition in which a truck was painted and decorated in the spirit of a moving art gallery. It journeyed across Pakistan.
4   6th National Exhibition of Visual Arts, National Art Gallery, Islamabad
3   Printmaking exhibition, American Center, Karachi

SIM AKHTAR

7   Born in Rawalpindi, Pakistan
7   Graduated in English Literature and Economics, Government College, Lahore
2   Bachelors in Textile Design, National College of Arts, Lahore

WORK EXPERIENCE
2003- Adjunct Faculty Member, Deptt. Of Fine Arts, Fatima Jinnah Women's University, Rawalpindi
2002   Curator, 'An Idea of Perfection: National Exhibition of Photography', PNCA, The Alhamra, Lahore and The Arts Council, Karachi
1999   Co-curator, 'Matti Ki Sargoshi', ASNA, Frere Hall, Karachi
1998   Photo-documentation of Traditional Textiles, Tana Bana, Karachi
1997   Panelist, International Seminar on Traditional Textiles, Karachi
1998   Organiser, Finnish Cultural Week, Embassy of Finland, Islamabad
1997   Coordinator and Designer, 'Dissident Voices: Festival of French/Pakistani Documentaries', Alliance Francaise, Islamabad
1995 - Art critic, The News on Sunday, Lahore
1995   Photo-documentation, International Committee of the Red Cross, Quetta
1995   Production Design,. 'Indus-Europa', Alliance Francaise, Islamabad and Lahore
1994-95 Art critic, Newsline, Karachi
1994   Photo-documentation, Margalla Hills National Park, WWF, Islamabad
1994   Photo-documentation, Wildlife Conservation: Bar, Churmian and Chitral, WWF
1991-93 Art critic, The Herald, Karachi

Work appeared in Alliance (France), Himal (Nepal), Ceramics Technical (Australia), International Gallerie (India), The Frontier Post (Lahore), Spach (Islamabad), The Tribune (Islamabad), Dawn Gallery (Karachi), Libas International (Lahore), Natura (Lahore)

SELECTED EXHIBITIONS
2004   'Another Dawn', Rohtas Gallery, Islamabad
2004   'Celebrating the Northern Areas', The Art Councils, Islamabad, Quetta, Karachi
2003   Flags of Peace, Beach Luxury Hotel, Karachi
2003   'War against War', Hunerkada, Islamabad
2003   'Subterranean', Rohtas II, Lahore
2001   Vasl International Artists' Show, Amin Gulgee Gallery, Karachi
1999   'Remembering Zahoor', Zahoor-ul-Akhlaque Gallery, The NCA, Lahore
1996   'Regards Croises', Alliance Francaise, Islamabad, Karachi, Peshawar
1995   'The Offered Look', Alliance Francaise, Islamabad
1992   'Vistar', Maharat, Karachi
1990   FIAP Group Show, Belgium
1989   ASG Group Show, USIS, Islamabad, Lahore, Karachi

RESIDENCIES

2002   Researcher/Curator, Fukuoka Asian Art Museum, Fukuoka, Japan
2002   Artists' Retreat, Chitral, PNCA
2001   Vasl International Artists' Residency, Gaddani Beach
2000   Writer, Ledig House, Hudson Valley, New York, USA
2000   Writer, Ucross Foundation, Clearmont, Wyoming, USA

DAVID ALESWORTH

ART TRAINING:
Brooklands Technical College, UK 1974-1976
Epsom School Of Art and Design, UK 1976-1977
Wimbledon School Of Art, BA. Hons Fine Art Sculpture, UK 1977-1980
Picker Fellowship in Sculpture, Kingston University, Kingston-Upon -Thames, UK 1980-1981

EXPERIENCE:
Visiting lecturer, Kingston University Sculpture Dept., UK 1982
Lecturer Glasgow School of Art, UK Sculpture Dept & Foundation Year 1981-1983
Moved to Karachi, Pakistan, June 1988
Lecturer in Sculpture, Indus Valley School of Art & Architecture, Karachi 1989
Advisor, Art Syllabus revision for Sindh Board of Technical Education, Karachi. 1992
Act. Head of Fine Art Dept., Indus Valley School of Art & Architecture, Karachi 1993
Elected member of the Royal Society of British Sculptors R.B.S. 1994
Study tour of various Indian art schools, including, Baroda School of Art, N.I.D Ahmadabad, J.J. School Bombay. 1996
Coordinator Fine Art Dept. Indus Valley School of Art & Architecture, Karachi 1996-98
Head of Foundation, Indus Valley School of Art and Architecture, Karachi
Study tour of various Australian Art schools, including: RMIT Melbourne, Univ. of South Australia, Queensland Univ. of Technology ,Brisbane. 1999
Study tour of various French Art schools and institutions including Ecole de Beaux Art, Aix, & public artists groups in the south of France.   1999
Member Academic Council Beaconhouse National University 2002
Admissions Board member Ziauddin University 2003

SHOWS:
Guildford University, UK 1978
New Contemporaries ICA, Institute Of Contemporary Art, ACGB, London, UK   1978

G.L.A.A. Cannizaro Park, Wimbledon Common, UK 1978-1982

G.L.A.A. Hounslow Civic Centre, UK 1981

One person Show, Kingston University, UK 1981

Hayward Annual A.C.G.B., London UK 1982

One person Show, Glasgow School Of Art, UK 1983

Rufford Open Northern Arts, UK 1987

Ziggurat Gallery, Karachi 1992

Ziggurat Gallery, Karachi 1993

National Gallery, Islamabad 1993

6th National Exhibition Islamabad 1994
(Awarded Silver Medal for Sculpture)

7th National Exhibition Islamabad 1996

Art Caravan, Touring Exhibition, Pakistan 1994

Six Artists, Rohtas Gallery, Islamabad 1994

National College of Art Gallery, Lahore 1995

Pakistan National Council for the Arts Gallery, Islamabad 1995

Indus Gallery Karachi 1995

Indus Valley School of Art & Architecture Gallery 1995

Punjab Art Association, Al-Hamra Complex, Lahore 1995

Kunj Art Gallery, Karachi 1995-1996

Container 96: Copenhagen, Denmark 1996

Selected Pakistani Artists, Birmingham 1996

"City Flowers" Denmark, Video Project 1996

Group show, Rohtas Gallery, Islamabad 1996

"High, Low and In between", AN Gallery, Karachi 1997

"The Longer Now", AN Gallery, Karachi 1997

"Urban Voices" Art Fest '97, Sheraton Hotel, Karachi 1997

"Arz-e-Mauood ,The Promised Lands" Frere Hall Gardens
Interactive, collaborative Installation 1997

Karachi Contemporaries AN Gallery Karachi 1998

"Urban Voices" II Art Fest '98, Sheraton Hotel, Karachi 1998

"City Flowers 2" Denmark, Video Project 1998

Exhibition of Drawings, Cafe Blue, Karachi 1998

Selected, with Durriya Kazi to represent Pakistan at
The First Fukuoka Asian Art Trienniale, Japan 1999

Art Exchange programme with Durriya Kazi and Yusuf and Sons

Fukuoka Asian Art Trienniale, Fukuoka Japan 1999

Urban Voices 111, Karachi Sheraton Hotel,1999

The Millenium Show, Karachi Arts Council 1999

Selected, with Durriya Kazi, to represent Pakistan at
The Third Asia Pacific Triennale, Brisbane, Australia 1999

Collaboration with Michael Lin on Magnetic Writing/
Marching Ideas, IT Park Gallery, Taipei 1999

"Urban Voices III", Karachi Pakistan 1999

"Cityscapes", Galerie Sadequain, Karachi 1999

"The Millenium Art Show", Arts Council of Pakistan,
Karachi 1999

"Pakistan Another Vision" Brunei gallery, SOAS, UK touring
show   2000

Huddersfield, Oldham, "Victoria Gallery" Bath & "Hot Bath"
Gallery Bath.

"Kara Art 2000", Alliance Francaise, Karachi 2000

"The Experimental Space" in the 90's A.C.K. 2000

"Lines of Descent" The Family in Contemporary Asian Art

Noosa, Cairns, Perc Tucker, Bundaberg and Rockhampton
galleries.

QAG touring show, web site through QAG 2000-2001

"Takhti" Project 2001

"Kara-Art 2001", Alliance Francaise, Karachi 2001

"1St Karachi International Film Festival" (Signtology
collaborative digital Video) 2001

"Speaking Out" Canvas Gallery, Karachi 2001

"Kara Art 2002" Alliance Francaise 2002

Solo show, Canvas Gallery, Karachi, 2002

"Aar Paar-2", public art project, Delhi & Karachi 2002

"Dish Dhamaka" Amin Gulgee Gallery, Karachi 2003

8th National Exhibition, PNCA, Islamabad 2003

Herald Magazine, collaboration with Adnan Madani 2003

"Around the Miniature-2", Lahore 2003

"Peace with India" Lahore 2003

"24 Frames per Second" 3rd KaraFilm Festival, PIIA,
Karachi 2003

"Happiness" curator David Elliot, Mori Art Museum, Tokyo,
Japan 2003-2004

"The Other" curator Quddus Mirza, National Gallery of
Modern Art, Colaba , Mumbai, India. Feb 2005

CURATORSHIP:

Co-Curated Truck Art Exhibition for the Music Village of
Pakistan Festival, October Gallery, London. 1995

Co-Curated Truck exhibition at the New World Gallery,
Dusseldorf, Germany 1996

At the AN Gallery Karachi: 1997-1998

High Low & In Between

The Longer Now

Belinda Eaton Summer 1997

Faiza Butt, recent works

Spaces Within

Contemporary Urdu Cinema Posters

Recent Indus Graduates

Karachi Contemporaries part 1.

Jason Fox & Huma Bhabha

Belinda Eaton Summer 1998

Shahbaz Malik

American Club, Karachi, 2004·

WORK IN PUBLIC COLLECTIONS:

"Art caravan", Karachi Metropolitan Council, Karachi

"Heart Mahal", Fukuoka Asian Art Museum, Fukuoka,
Japan.

"Avation Fuel Tanker/collaboration", Pvt collection,
Fukuoka, Japan.

"Very Very Sweet Medina", Queensland Art Gallery,
Brisbane, Australia

WAJID ALI

EDUCATION:
2004: B.A. (Hons.) Fine Arts, Painting and Filmmaking,
Dept. of Visual Studies, University of Karachi

EXPERIENCE:
*Art Director, MANDUCK COLLECTIVES.
• Worked as Assistant Director, with Programme Director
Abuzar Khan.
• Worked with Japanese Consulate as visual artist.
• Programme Director, THE CARROT COMPANY.

EXHIBITIONS:
2001 Photography Exhibition, Frere Hall, Karachi.
2001 Quaid-e-Azam Photography Exhibition, University
of Karachi.
2002 Group Show, Forum, Karachi.
2002 Group Show, "Aaj Ki Aurat', University of Karachi.
2004 Group Show, "Art Extravaganza", Pearl Continent
Hotel, Karachi.
2004 Thesis Display, Dept. of Visual Studies, University
of Karachi.
2005 Group Show, "Emerging Talent", V.M.Gallery,
Karachi.
2005 Group Show, Alliance de Frances, Karachi.

ACHIEVEMENTS:
Rangoonwala Scholarship Award for 2004.
Certificates in sports and extra curricular activities.

SHAH MURAD ALIANI

MUSIC:
• Compose and produce music with an associate under the
entity "Ustaaz"
• Ustaaz to its credit has successfully undertaken various
projects, namely:
• Original Soundtrack for "Beauty Parlor"
• Original 40 minute music piece in 4 different segments
highlight a fashion show celebrating the 50th Anniversary
of Pakistan held in Mauritius.
• 15 minute original music segment for Khaddi's show held
for Jinnah Foundation in 2000.
• More than 30 minutes of original music made for Amin
Gulgee's show entitled " Alchemy".
• More than 30 minutes of original music made for Amin
Gulgee's 2nd show entitled " Sola Singhar".
• Lux Style Award theme.
• Original soundtracks to telefilms/plays: " Aur Zindagi
Badalti hai", "Kahaneeyan" (nominated in KARA film
festival for best original score) and various others.
• Have compiled music for various other fashion shows.
• Currently, DJ twice a week, every Tuesday and Thursday

ght on CityFM 89.

ERESTS:
igital Photography
yokushinkai (Japanese Martial Art)
Weight Training & Nutrition
ogs
ricket

FAT ALVI

ESENT EMPLOYMENT:
Director / Curator, V.M. Art Gallery, Since 1987
MG Rangoonwala Community Centre, Dhoraji Society,
      Karachi 74800, Pakistan.

T EDUCATION:
73   Graduation in Fine Arts with Design as Subsidiary
      Subject from Karachi School of Art.

STINCTIONS:
05   Pride of Accomplishment Award K.S.A.
00   Chosen Ambassador for Asia Continent in UNO by
      Common Ground World Project, New York USA.
88   Shield for Best Water color, Osaka, Japan.
74   2nd Prize Exhibition ?74, at USSR Consulate,
      Karachi.
73   1st Prize All Pakistan Poster and Car Sticker
      Competition.

HOLARSHIPS BURSARIES:
95-97 Cultural Scholarship, Goethe Institute, Berlin,
      Germany.
93-94 Visiting artist By British Council Commonwealth
      Institute, U.K.
91   National Art Gallery Harare, Zimbabwe.
90   Pakistan German Forum, Exhibition of Painting /
      Slide Talk on Craft of Pakistan. Germany
86   From ITC/UNCTAD, GATT Geneva, and UNO
      Project. For Development of Pakistan Handicrafts
      Design Research Work USA.

TIST RESIDENCY:
00   Izmir International Ceramic Symposium Invitation
      to Dokuz Aylul University, Fine Art Faculty, Ceramic
      Department, Turkey.
98   IPHO Art Festival Malaysia invited by Art
      Foundation.
97   UNESCO Asian Artist Workshop / Residency, Iran.
96   Artist Residency, Breton Hall, College of the
      University of Leeds, UK.

LECTED SOLO EXHIBITIONS:
005 'Search Within' Solo scheduled at Canvas Gallery,

      Karachi.
2003 'Fire & Earth' Solo at Zeniani Gallery, Karachi.
1998 'Cradle of Love Series', Nomad Gallery at Institute
      of craft and Cultural Activities Islamabad (Media
      Earth).
1996 'Dust To Dust II' Media Earth, Lawrence Bartley
      Gallery, Britton Hall, Wakefield, UK.
1995 'Dust to Dust' Media Natural Earth, V.M. Art
      Gallery Karachi, Pakistan.
1993 'Lost Civilization', Natural Earth, Commonwealth,
      Institute, U.K.
1991 'Forgotten Cities' (Water Color) National Art
      Gallery, Harare, Zimbabwe.
1990 'Moenjodaro', (acrylic), Zeilitzheim, Germany.
1989 'Dua Series', (Graphite), Gallery Chowkandi,
      Karachi Pakistan.

SELECTED INTERNATIONAL GROUP SHOWS:
2003 'flags of peace' traveling exhibition, south East Asia
2000 Invited to Common Ground World Project
      Inauguration Ceremony UN Head Quarters New
      York USA (Participated as the Ambassador for
      continent of Asia). (Catalogued)
2000 Ceramic exhibition, National State Gallery Izmir,
      Turkey. (Catalogued)
2000 'Another Vision', Pakistani painter Traveling
      exhibition to London, Huddersfield, Glasgow,
      Bathe, U.K. (Catalogued)
1996 11th Asia International Water Color Exhibition
      Kuala Lumpur, Petronas Gallery Malaysia
      Exhibition. (Catalogued)
1997 Asia Women Artists Workshop / Exhibition
      Nairawan Art Gallery Tehran, Iran. (Catalogued)
1996 Birendra Gallery, Khatmandu, Nepal.
1996 SAARC Country Show New Delhi India.
1989 Permanent Collection Show Non-aligned Gallery,
      Zimbabwe.
1988 Asian Art Biennale, Dhaka, Bangladesh.
      (Catalogued)
1980 Asian Painters Exhibition of Painting Fukouka,
      Japan. (Catalogued)

INLAND GROUP SHOWS:
50 group shows, from 1973 to 2005, 8 National exhibitions.

CURATORIAL EXPERIENCES:
1987-2005 Curated several National and International
      shows, in Netherlands, France, China, Australia,
      Turkey, UK, Japan, USA, Poland, Italy, Malaysia, Sri
      Lanka and many other countries.

PRIVATE COLLECTION:
      Pakistan, U.K, USA, India, Germany, Canada,
      China, Japan, Nepal, Arab Emirates, Museum of

contemporary Art Tehran, Iran, Singapore, France,
Sweden,Turkey, Zimbabwe, Kenya.

NAAZISH ATA-ULLAH

EDUCATION:
Reading for Ph.D. in Art Education at Institute of Education,
      University of London, concurrent with professional
      practice and teaching.
1984-85 Post-graduate studies in Printmaking
      The Slade School of Fine Art, University of London
1985 Art Teachers Certificate (post-graduate
      qualification) Institute of Education, University of
      London
1983 National Diploma in Fine Art, National College of
      Arts, Lahore.
1969 Bachelor of Arts, University of the Punjab, Kinnaird
      College for Women, Lahore.

AWARDS/FELLOWSHIPS:
1997 Conferred Associateship of the National College
      of Arts by the Fellows of the NCA for services
      rendered to the College
1995-96 The Charles Wallace Pakistan Trust award for
      research.
1992-97 Overseas Research Students Award 1992 – 97,UK
1988 Prize in Graphics. First Pakistan Art Biennial, Al
      Hamra Art Centre, Lahore.
1984-85 British Council Scholarship.
1969 Merit Scholarship in BA, Punjab University.

TEACHING:
1985 · Appointed in the Department of Fine Art, National
      College of Arts (NCA), Lahore. Incharge of
      Printmaking. Currently Associate Professor
In addition to teaching responsibilities in the under-
      graduate programme, appointed Course Tutor
      for MA(Hons) Visual Art (1998). Member of
      a committee that developed a post-graduate
      programme in the Department of Fine Art; duties
      entailed: planning and developing the programme
      including developing curricula.
Re-organized and established the Printmaking Studio at
      NCA (1985). Designed syllabuses for the BA degree
      in Printmaking.
Teach intaglio, planographic and relief printing methods
      to students of 2nd, 3rd and 4th years of the
      Department of Fine Art and the Faculty of Design,
      NCA. Tutor students of Sculpture, Painting and
      Miniature Painting on regular basis.
Conducted and co-ordinated several workshops, lectures
      and seminars in the Printmaking Studio specifically
      and in other areas at NCA. These include: the
      International Seminar on Art, Architecture and

Design Education in the New Millenium, in connection with the College's 125th Anniversary Celebrations; an international workshop on traditional, natural dyes (sponsored by UNESCO) in the Textiles Department, (1998); a workshop on etching by Joaquin Capa Eiriz sponsored by the Spanish Embassy (1998); a workshop on the conservation of archival materials (sponsored by The British Council), (1997); the International Art Workshop comprising thirteen visiting artists (sponsored by Cupola International, the Japan Foundation and The British Council), (1996);a series of six lectures by Robert Skelton (former Keeper of the Indian Section at the Victoria and Albert Museum) on Miniature Painting (1989); a workshop in lithography with Mr. Peter Daglish, Chelsea School of Art, and The Slade School of Fine Art, London, (1987); a workshop in etching with Professor Bartolomeu dos Santos, former Head, Department of Printmaking, The Slade School of Fine Art, London, (1986); a workshop on paper-making with Agnes Olive, Canadian artist (1986).

1998- Member and current Chairperson NCA Library Committee.
1985 Taught painting and drawing at Brixton College of Further Education, London
1984 Conducted children's art workshop in the Walled City of Lahore.

EXHIBITIONS:
2005 "Beyond Borders: Art of Pakistan", National Gallery of Modern Art, Mumbai
2004-5 "Contemporary Printmakers From Pakistan", Highpoint Center for Printmaking, Minneapolis; at the Catherine J. Smith Gallery, Appalachian State University in Boone
The Tatkhti Exhibition at the Missisauga Art Museum, Toronto, Canada
2003 "Darmiyaan" artists' workshop, Neherghar, Lahore
"Threads, Dreams, Desires" Harris Museum, Preston, UK; as part of exhibition from Pakistan
"Let Peace Prevail" Pakistani Women Artists at the V.M. Gallery, Karachi
2002 Break on Through to The Other Side/ A Cyber-sent Art Exhibition of Contemporary Art From Pakistan
The Takhti Exhibition, curated by the Takhti Curatorial Committee for the Zahoor ul Akhlaq Collective Trust, Sadequain Gallery, Frere Hall, Karachi
2000 Solo Show of Paintings at SimSim Gallery, Lahore
White on White, Group show at the Rohtas Gallery, Islamabad
Southwards From The Silk Road, Didrichsen Art Museum, Finland. (Curated contemporary

paintings and miniatures from Pakistan for the show)
2000 Pakistan Another Vision: Fifty Years of Painting and Sculpture from Pakistan; opened at the Brunei Gallery, London, travelled to the Huddersfield Art Gallery, the Oldham Art Gallery and the Victoria Art Gallery in Bath
2000 Remembering Zahoor, Zahoor ul Akhlaq Gallery, National College of Arts, Lahore
1999 The Quartersaw Gallery, Portland Oregon, USA
Scope VIII Zahoor ul Akhlaq Gallery, National College of Arts, Lahore
Art in the Time of Zahoor at the Rohtas Gallery, Islamabad
Printmakers from Pakistan, Cartwright Hall, Bradford, England. (Co-Curator of the Exhibition and wrote the Brochure entry)
1997 Scope VII National College of Arts, Lahore.
1994-96 An Intelligent Rebellion, Exhibition of Women Artists From Pakistan, Cartwright Hall, Bradford England; at UNESCO Headquarters, Paris 1995; and in other locations in Britain for two years.

Scope V. National College of Arts, Lahore.
1991 Group Show, Rohtas Gallery, Islamabad.
1991 Punjab Exhibition, Alhamra Art Centre, Lahore.
1991 Eight Contemporaries, Nairang Gallery, Lahore.
1991 Three Pakistani Women Artists, Centre For Contemporary Art, New Delhi.
1991 Group Show, Rohtas Gallery, Islamabad.
1990 A Representative Exhibition of Graphic Prints, National Gallery, Islamabad.
1989 "The Colors of Spring" Exhibition of Women Artists, National Gallery, Islamabad.
1989 4th Asian Art Biennial, Dhaka, as part of Pakistan's exhibition.
1988 Solo exhibition of Prints, Rohtas Gallery, Islamabad.
1988 Two-Person Show of Etchings with Anwar Saeed, Chawkandi Gallery, Karachi.
1988 Third International Exhibition (AIFACS) New Delhi.
1988 First Pakistan Art Biennial, Alhamra Art Gallery, Lahore.
1987 "Contemporary Art from Pakistan", ICIS Gallery, London.
1987 "Seven Artists from Pakistan", Kunstnersenter, Oslo, Norway.
1987 "The Art of Printmaking", Exhibition and Seminar, National Gallery, Islamabad.
1986 "Group 86", Chawkandi Gallery Karachi.
1985 Group Show, Rohtas Gallery, Islamabad.
1985 Established own studio with facilities for painting and etching.
1983 Group Show, Rohtas Gallery, Islamabad.
Participated in three National Exhibitions.

CONSULTANCY:
2004-5 Design consultant for the refurbishment of the Governor's house, NWFP
2002- 4 Participant in a three-year project on 'Modernity and National Identity in Art 1860-1940: India, Japan and Mexico'; conducted by the University Sussex (Prof.Partha Mitter), The Chelsea School of Art (Prof. Toshio Watanabe) and the Camberw School of Art (Prof. Oriana Baddeley).
2003- 4 Academic advisor and Member Academic Committee, School of Visual Art and School of Design and Architecture, Beaconhouse National University, Lahore
Prepared a proposal for the Alhamra Arts Centre Lahore, for the setting up of a Printmaking Workshop on its premises.
Designed and taught four courses on women's art at the Institute of Women's Studies Lahore. Member of faculty at IWSL.
1998-03 Member of the Board of ASR. ASR is a not for profit organisation working for social research an the education of women.
1997- Chair, Board of Directors, Bunyad Literacy Community Council. Bunyad is a not for profit organisation working for women's literacy and basic education for girls in rural Pakistan.
1994 Education consultant to the Pakistan School of Fashion Design, Lahore, for which I prepared the foundation course.
1994 Conducted workshop in the Walled City, Lahore, Hawwa Associates and Unifem.
1991 Designer for interior of The British Council, Laho
1989 Honorary advisor to the Shakir Ali Museum for establishment of a Printmaking Workshop at the Museum.
Director and honorary education consultant to the Lahore Society for Education and Research. The Society runs two schools; namely the Lahore School of Arts and Sciences and the Lahore Colle of Arts and Sciences (LACAS).
1984 Co-designer of mural at Tabaq Restaurant, Lahor (with Zahoor ul Akhlaq)
1983-84 Co-designer of monument at Tarbela Dam

ALI AZMAT

EDUCATION
MFA (Gold Medal) Dept of Fine Arts, University of Punjab, 1998
BFA, Dept of Fine Arts, University of Punjab, 1997
2 year Diploma in drawing and painting from Alhamra Academy of Performing Arts, Lahore, 1994

SOLO EXHIBITIONS

...vas Gallery, Karachi, 2005
...vas gallery, Karachi, 2003 (Preview at STUDIO A,
    Lahore,
...il 2003)
...wings' Exhibition, Alhamra Art Gallery, Lahore, 1999

...OUP EXHIBITIONS
...rtists from Lahore at Tariq Jay Art Galley, Karachi 2002
...rtists at Canvas gallery, Karachi, 2001
...z gallery, Lahore 2001
...z Gallery, Lahore, 2000
...ennium Show, Ejaz Gallery, Lahore, 2000
...sis Exhibition, Anna Molka Gallery, Lahore, 1999
...amra Art Gallery, Lahore, 1999
...age of Pakistan", World Bank, Islamabad, 2004
...ibition of International Interchange of MOK WOD HOE
    Art Association, Spirit of Asia, Korea, 2003
...j Art Gallery, Karachi, 2003
...hti Exhibition, Gallerie Sadequain, Frere Hall, Karachi,
    2001
...xpressions 2K", District Administration, Jhelum, 2001
...rticipated in all exhibitions held by Punjab Artists
    Association and Young Artists Association (1994
    to date)

...PERIENCE
...iting lecturer, painting, since 1999 at College of Art and
    Design, University of Punjab, Lahore
...rtoonist, illustrator and contributor for "The Nation",
    Pakistan, 1998-1999
...ustrated children's stories for Tabeer Publishers, 1997-
    1998

...WARDS
...ational Excellence Award, presented by the Pakistan
    National Council of theArts, at the 5th National
    Exhibition, 2003
...vard of Honour, presented by the Artists Association of
    Punjab, at their 14th Annual Exhibition, 1999
...d Prize in the Annual Alhamra Student's Painting
    Competition presided by Lahore Arts Council, 1997
...d prize, Painting Competition by Daily Jung, Lahore,
    1996
...old Medal in MFA, Dept of Fine Arts, University of Punjab,
    2000
...esented a shield by Civil Services Academy, Lahore, 2001
...d Prize in Painting, by Directorate General of Social
    welfare, Women Development, Govt. of Punjab,
    Lahore, 2001

KRAM DOST BALOCH

...DUCATION:
...A. Fine Arts, National College, Lahore.

PRESENT POSITION:
Assistant Professor, Fine Arts Department, University of
    Baluchistan, Quetta
Member, Board of Governors, National College of Arts,
    Lahore

NATIONAL AWARDS:
Presidential Award (Pride of Performance)
Bolan Award
Best Artist Award, Balouchistan Arts Council
National Award, P.N.C.A, Islamabad
Red Crescent Award, Islamabad
Gold Medal Award, Bolan Cultural Society, Lahore

SELECT SOLO EXHIBITIONS:
Alliance Française, Islamabad
Art Gallery, Quetta
Art Gallery, Islamabad
Clifton Art Gallery, Karachi
Alliance Française, Islamabad
Rothas Gallery, Islamabad
Nairang Gallery, Lahore
Balouch Club, Bahrain
Canvas Gallery, Karachi

SELECT GROUP SHOWS:
Chawkandi Gallery, Karachi
7th Biennale, Dhaka, Bangladesh
"Tempered Surface," Oldham Art Galleries, Oldham, UK
P.N.C.A Exhibition, National Gallery, Islamabad
5th National Exhibition, P.N.C.A, Lahore
4th National Exhibition, P.N.C.A, Lahore
Rothas Gallery, Islamabad

WORKSHOPS:
VASL International Workshop, Gadani, Balochistan
Workshop Residence at the Paris Expo
Pakistan Pavilion, Nagoya, Japan

PUBLIC COLLECTIONS:
Staff College, Quetta, Mural Painting
Chief Minister House, Quetta
Governor House, Quetta
President House, Islamabad
N.A,B, Islamabad
French Embassy, Islamabad
UNESCO Head Office, Paris

CREATIVE CONSTRUCTION:
15-foot pavilion designed and constructed at Lok Virsa,
    Islamabad

NOORJEHAN BILGRAMI

ACADEMICS
2001-02 Japan Foundation Fellowship, Tama Art
    University, Tokyo
1972-74 Diploma in Fine Art, Central Institute of Arts &
    Crafts, Karachi
1968-69 National College of Arts, Lahore
1968 Cambridge University, 'A' Levels, Karachi Grammar
    School
1966 Cambridge University, 'O' Levels, Karachi Grammar
    School

PROFESSIONAL EXPERIENCE
2005 National Consultant for Pakistan, UNIDO, Vienna
2004 Curator, Exhibition of Traditional Textiles,"
    Tana Bana: The Woven Soul of Pakistan", Nihon
    Mingeikan, The Japan Folk Craft Museum, Tokyo
2003 Co-Curator, Exhibition of Traditional Textiles," Tana
    Bana: The Woven Soul of Pakistan", Pacific Asia
    Museum, Pasadena, California.
2000- Landscape Design Consultant
1999 Curator, Exhibition of Traditional Textiles," Tana
    Bana: The Woven Soul of Pakistan", Pacific
    Northwest College of Art, Portland, Oregon
1998 Co-Curator, Exhibition of Traditional Textiles,
    " Tana Bana: The Woven Soul of Pakistan",
    University of Wisconsin, Madison
1997 Co-Curator, Exhibition of Traditional Textiles, Indus
    Valley School of Art & Architecture, Karachi
1996-97 Honorary Head, Department of Fine Art, Indus
    Valley School of Art & Architecture, Karachi
1991-96 Executive Director, Indus Valley School of Art &
    Architecture, Karachi
1978 - Established KOEL, House of Block Printed Fabrics,
    Embroidery & Weaves
1976-78 Color Consultant, Paintex Ltd. (ICI Group of
    Companies), Karachi
1974-77 Senior School Art Teacher, Convent of Jesus &
    Mary, Karachi
1970-72 Senior School Art Teacher, Convent of Jesus &
    Mary, Karachi

EXHIBITIONS OF PAINTINGS
2004 Solo Exhibition, "Unbleached Mark", Canvas
    gallery, Karachi 2004
2003 8th National Exhibition of Visual Arts, Alhambra,
    Lahore
2002 Group Show, "A Tribute to Ali Imam", Indus Gallery,
    Karachi
2001 Commissioned Paintings for Allied Bank of
    Pakistan, Presidential floor, Karachi
2000 Group Show, "Art Fest 2000", Sheraton Hotel &
    Towers, Karachi
1999 Group Show, "Art Fest 99", Sheraton Hotel &

Towers, Karachi

1999 Solo Exhibition, Quartersaw Gallery, Portland, Oregon, USA
1999 Group Show, Chawkandi Art Gallery, Karachi
1998 Group Show, "Urban Voices 98", Sheraton Hotel & Towers, Karachi
1998 Group Show, Momart Art Gallery, Karachi
1997 Group Show "Inspiration", American Centre, Karachi
1996 7th National Exhibition of Visual Arts, Islamabad
1995 Group Show of Drawings, Momart Art Gallery, Karachi
1995 "An Intelligent Rebellion", Women Artists of Pakistan Travelling Exhibition, UK
1995 Solo Exhibition "Black Silence", Chawkandi Art Gallery, Karachi
1995 Group Show, Indus Gallery, Karachi
1994 PNCA Travelling Exhibition of Pakistani Artists through the Middle East
1994 6th National Exhibition of Visual Arts, Islamabad
1992 Solo Exhibition, Chawkandi Art Gallery, Karachi
1992 Women Painters' Exhibition, American Centre, Karachi
1991 All Pakistan Women Painters' Exhibition, National Art Gallery, Islamabad
1990 Group Show, The Gallery, Islamabad
1987 Biennale Pakistan Painters, National Art Gallery, Islamabad
1987 Solo Exhibition "Crying for the Light", Indus Gallery, Karachi
1974-86 Participated in several Group Shows in Karachi, Lahore and Islamabad

MOEEN FARUQI

SOLO EXHIBITIONS:
Khas Gallery, Islamabad, 2005
Zenaini Gallery, Karachi, 2004
Croweaters Gallery, Lahore, 2003
Chawkandi Art Gallery, Karachi, 2002
Gallery Pangloss, Pisa, Italy, 2000
The Art Gallery, Islamabad 1999
Indus Gallery, Karachi, 1998
Chawkandi Art Gallery, Karachi,1997
Indus Gallery, Karachi, 1995
Indus Gallery, Karachi, 1993

GROUP SHOWS:
The Art Gallery of Peel, Brampton, Ontario, 2001
Lakeshore Arts, Toronto, 2001
Gallery 401, Toronto, July 2001
SAVAC Exhibition, Interaccess Gallery, Toronto, 2001
Canvas Gallery, Karachi, 2000
The Millenium Show, Arts Council of Pakistan, 1999

Urban Voices, Sheraton Art Festival, Karachi, 1997, 1998, 1999
Asian Art Biennale, Dhaka, Bangladesh, 1997
Artists from Karachi, Hunerkada, Islamabad, 1996
National Art Exhibition, Pakistan National Council of the Arts, Islamabad, 1996
National Art Exhibition, Alhamra Arts Centre, 1995
PNCA, Islamabad, 1995
National College of Arts, Lahore, 1994
6th Asia Watercolor Exhibition, Nagoya, Japan, 1991
Shakir Ali Museum, Lahore, 1990

POETRY
Poems have been published in *Poetry from Pakistan: An Anthology*, Oxford University Press (1997) and in *Dragonfly in the Sun: An Anthology of Pakistani Literature*, Oxford University Press (1997), Karachi. Poems have also appeared in *Verse*, *Orbis*, *The Rialto* (UK), *Rattle* (USA) and in *Cyphers* (Ire.).

AMIN GULGEE

EDUCATION:
B.A. in Economics and Art History, Yale University, New Haven, CT, USA, 1987
Recipient of Cogar B. Goodyear Fine Arts Award for Thesis on Moghul Gardens

EXHIBITIONS (SOLO):
Canvas Gallery, Karachi, Pakistan 2004
Townhouse Gallery, Kuala Lumpur, Malaysia 2004
Art Space, Dubai, UAE 2004
Museu da Agua, Lisbon, Portugal 2003
Open Studio IV: 'Char Bagh,' Karachi, Pakistan 2003
Open Studio! III, Karachi, Pakistan 2000
The Gallery of the IMF, Washington DC, USA 1999-2000 (catalogue)
The Soni Gallery, London, UK 1999
The Peterborough Museum, Peterborough, UK 1999
The Arabian Gallery, Dubai, UAE 1999
Art Gallery, Islamabad, Pakistan 1999
Ankara Hilton, Ankara, Turkey 1998
Occidental College, Los Angeles, USA 1998
The Soni Gallery, London, UK 1998
Second International Conference on Islamic Unity, Washington, DC, USA 1998
Open Studio II, Karachi, Pakistan 1998
The Ismaili Centre, London, UK 1997
Jordan National Gallery, Amman, Jordan 1997 (catalogue)
Open Studio I, Karachi, Pakistan 1997
Paramount Studios, Los Angeles, USA 1996
The Galleria, Houston, USA 1996
Lahore Art Gallery, Lahore, Pakistan 1996
Hofstra University, Hempstead, NY, USA 1996

Embassy of Pakistan, Paris, France 1995
Benefit for UNICEF (opened by Mrs. Boutros Boutros Ghali), New York, USA 1994
Commonwealth Institute (opened by Prime Minister Benazir! Bhutto), London, UK 1994
Parliament House (opened by Prime Minister Benazir Bhutto), Islamabad, Pakistan 1994
Rida Gallery, Jeddah, Saudi Arabia 1994
Al-Nahda Royal Society, Riyadh, Saudi Arabia 1994
Meridian International Center, Washington, DC, USA 199
United Nations, New York, USA 1992
Zenith Gallery, Washington, DC, USA 1992
The Art Gallery, Islamabad, Pakistan 1992
Lahore Art Gallery, Lahore, Pakistan 1992
Inter-Continental Hotel, Muscat, Oman 1991
Inter-Continental Hotel, Dubai, UAE 1991
Indus Gallery, Karachi, Pakistan 1990
Zenith Gallery, Washington, DC, USA 1989
Embassy of Pakistan, Washington, DC, USA 1989
The Lawrence Gallery, New York, USA 1989
Pakistan American Cultural Center, Karachi, Pakistan 198

GROUP SHOWS:
'18 at 8,' Wei-Ling Gallery, Kuala Lumpur, Malaysia 2005 (catalogue)
'Beyond Borders,' National Gallery of Modern Art, Mumba India 2005 (catalogue)
'Old Masters, Young Voices,' Al-Hamra Gallery, Lahore, Paksitan 2004
Beijing Biennale, Beijing, China 2003 (catalogue)
The Kufa Gallery, London, UK 2002
KaraArt, Alliance Française, Karachi, Pakistan 2002
The Uraan Project, The Amin Gulgee Gallery, Karachi, Pakistan 2002 (catalogue)
The Takhti Project, Gallerie Sadequain, Karachi, Pakistan 2001 (catalogue)
VASL, The Amin Gulgee Gallery, Karachi, Pakistan 2001 (catalogue)
KaraArt, Alliance Française, Karachi, Pakistan 2001
Pakistan: Another Vision, Brunei Gallery, London, UK 200 (catalogue)
Qal'm: An Exhibition of Calligraphy, Mohatta Palace Museum, Karachi, Pakistan 2000
KaraArt, Alliance Française, Karachi, Pakistan 2000
Millennium Show, Arts Council of Pakistan, Karachi, Pakistan 2000
Pakistan Pavilion, Expo, Hanover, Germany 2000
1999 Group Show, Chawkandi Gallery, Karachi, Pakistan 1999
Open: ! Prima Esposizione Internazionale di Sculture al Lido, Venice, Italy 1998 (catalogue)
Contemporary Artists from India and Pakistan, Gallerie Martini, Hong Kong, PRC 1997
50 Years of Art in Pakistan, The Connoisseur Gallery,

London, UK 1997
Eighth Asia Biennial, Dhaka, Bangladesh 1997
gural Show, The WAH Center, Brooklyn, NY, USA 1996
temporary Moslem Artists, Hofstra University,
    Hempstead. NY, USA 1996 (catalogue)
Boston, USA 1989
Wave Gallery, New Haven, CT, USA 1988

MMISSIONS:
ps,' Parliament House Entrance, Islamabad, Pakistan
e Message," The Presidency, Islamabad, Pakistan
nar," Quaid-e-Azam International Airport, Karachi,
    Pakistan
bitat," The Aga Khan Center, Houston, USA
ar Bagh," The Serena Hotel, Islamabad, Pakistan
an and Computer," IBM Museum, Karachi, Pakistan
lance," BASF, Karachi, Pakistan
ah," Marriot Hotel, Isla! mabad, Pakistan
be," Citibank Gold Office, Lahore, Pakistan
fi," Aga Khan Foundation, New York, USA

BLIC COLLECTIONS:
e International Monetary Fund, Washington, DC, USA
dan National Gallery, Amman, Jordan
fstra University Museum, Hempstead, NY, USA
e WAH Center, Brooklyn NY, USA
kistan Modern Art Museum, Islamabad, Pakistan

SHION SHOWS/PERFORMANCE ART PIECES:
handara,' Pakistan Pavilion, Expo, Nagoya, Japan
in Gulgee's Sola Singhar, Sheraton Hotel, Karachi,
    Pakistan 2001
in Gulgee's Alchemy, Sheraton Hotel, Karachi, Pakistan,
    2000
welry for Mary McFadden's 1996 Spring/Summer
    Collection, Fashion Week: Seventh on Fifth, New
    York Public Library, New York, USA

JRATORIAL WORK:
ban Voices V, Sheraton Hotel, Karachi, Pakistan 2001
ban Voices IV, Sheraton Hotel, Karachi, Pakistan 2000
ban Voices III, Sheraton Hotel, Karachi, Pakistan 1999
ban Voices II, Sheraton Hotel, Karachi, Pakistan 1998
ban Voices, Sheraton Hotel, Karachi, Pakistan 1997

VARDS:
resident's Pride of Performance, 2005
ung Achiever Award, Indus Vision, 2001
rst Award for Jewelry, Pakistan School of Fashion Design,
    2001
alligraph-Art Award, Second International Calligraphy
    and Calligrapha-Art Exhibition and Competition,
    Lahore, Pakistan 1999
xcellence in Art Award, Sindh Government, 1993

SHEHERBANO HUSSAIN

EDUCATION
1996   Extended Studies in Metaphysics, Texas A&M
        University, College Station, USA
1995   BFA (Painting & Printmaking), Indus Valley School
        of Art & Architecture, Karachi

EXPERIENCE
08 05–present Lecturer, Art Theory, Indus Valley School
        of Art
07 97–present Freelance Art Critic, Newsline, Karachi
09 03–05 05 Lecturer, Painting, University of Karachi
10 02–12 03 Juror, Karafilmfest
01 00–11 00 Volunteer for the Human Rights Education
        Program magazine, "Aware"
10 99–02 00 Script editing and narration in english for a
        documentary, titled, "Forests of Sindh"
01 96–04 02 Visiting Faculty, Indus Valley School of Art
08 95–10 97 Freelance Illustrator, Book Group, Karachi

CURATORIAL EXPERIENCE
2006   "Renaissance: New Voices in Islamic Calligraphy",
        co-curated with Amin Gulgee, Amin Gulgee Gallery,
        Karachi
2006   "The Body Beyond the Nude", co-curated with Amin
        Gulgee, Amin Gulgee Gallery, Karachi
2001   Curatorial committee member, "Takhti Exhibition",
        Frere Hall, Karachi

SELECT EXHIBITIONS
2005   Earthquake Relief Show, Nomad Gallery,
        Islamabad.
2003   "Flags of Peace", Beach Luxury Hotel, Karachi
2003   Solo exhibition, Dubai, UAE
2002   Solo exhibition, Chawkandi Gallery, Karachi
2002   "Uraan Exhibition", Amin Gulgee Gallery, Karachi
2001   "JCAT/2001 Arts Tour", First Street Loft, Jersey
        City, USA
2001   Solo exhibition, Zenaini Gallery, Karachi
1999   Engro Group Show, Dharki, Sindh
1998   "Karachi Contemporaries", A.N.Gallery, Coconut
        Grove, Karachi
1997   Two person show, Frere Hall, Karachi
1996   Juried Art Show, Brazos Valley Art League, Texas,
        USA
1996   7th Annual Exhibition, Pakistan National Council of
        Arts, Islamabad

TELEVISION INTERVIEWS
2004   PTV, Pakistan
2001   PTV, Pakistan
1998   NTM, Pakistan

AWARDS
1996   1st Prize, Juniour Artists Category, Brazos Centre,
        Texas, USA
1989   1st Prize, Student's Exhibition, PACC, Karachi
        (Juried by Ali Imam)

Website: www.geocities.com/sheherbanohussain

TAPU JAVERI

SELECTED EXHIBITIONS
2001   Kara Art, Alliance Francaise Gallery, Karachi
2001   Takhti Exhibition, Galerie Sadequain, Karachi
2001   Photography as Art, Arts Council, Karachi
2001   Capturing Moments, Freezing Truths, British
        Council, Karachi
2000   Art Gallery, Islamabad
2000   Kara Art, Alliance Francaise Gallery, Karachi
2000   Croweaters Gallery, Lahore
2000   Pakistan American Cultural Center, Karachi
2000   Art Fest, hotel Sheraton, Karachi
2000   The Experimental Space, Arts Council, Karachi
1999   Art Fest, Hotel Sheraton, Karachi
1999   Canvas Gallery, Karachi
1999   Millenium Show, Arts Council, Karachi
1998   Urban Voices II, Art Fest, Hotel Sheraton, Karachi
1997   Pakistan American Cultural Center, Karachi
1997   Urban Voices, Art Fest, Hotel Sheraton, Karachi
1997   Indus Gallery, Karachi
1985   Pakistan American Cultural Center, Karachi
1985   Visually Speaking, Arts Council, Karachi

AUJ KHAN

EDUCATION
Bachelor of Fine Arts, 2003
Indus Valley School of Art and Architecture.
Painting and Photography

EXHIBITIONS
Painting Exhibit at Duriya Kazi's City Display, Frere Hall,
        Karachi, 2002
Photography Exhibit with Farah Mahbub, IVSA, 2003.
Portrait Photography Exhibit, Arts Council Karachi, 2003.
Degree Show, Indus Valley School, 2003
'Emerging Talent', VM Art Gallery, 2004
International Rotaract Peace Festival Showing, 2004
Kara Art Festival, Sheraton 2004
'Suspension of Disbelief' Kara Film Festival, Pakistan
        Institute of International Affairs, Karachi 2004
'Taaza Tareen' VASL Residency Connections I, Karachi,
        April 2005 http://www.vaslart.org/aujk.html
'Voices' Group Show World Bank Office Islamabad, April

2005
'Opportunities' VM ART Gallery Group Show, May 2005
AIWA;International Artists Workshop, Aley, Lebanon,
   September 2005
Group Show, Rohtas Gallery, Islamabad, November 2005
Kara Film Festival, Pakistan Institute of International
   Affairs, Karachi 2005

TEACHING
Indus Valley School of Art and Architecture
Fine Art Department 2003-2004
Karachi University, Visual Art Department 2005
Citizens Foundation Schools Volunteer Program 2005

WORKING MEMBER
VASL Pakistan, Triangle Arts Trust UK
International Residency and Workshops for Artists 2004
   -2006

AWARDS
WWF All Pakistan Art Competition, 1st Prize,
Al Hamra Lahore
IVSA Distinction in Thesis Award
IVSA Over all Distinction Award

NAIZA KHAN

EDUCATION
1987-90 University of Oxford, Somerville College Oxford
           Ruskin School of Drawing and Fine Art
           Bachelor degree in Fine Art
1986-87 Wimbledon School of Art London
           Art Foundation Course

SOLO EXHIBITIONS
2004   Exhale Canvas Gallery Karachi
2000   Voices Merge Chawkandi Art Karachi
1995   La Linea Negra Gallery 7 Hong Kong
1993   Chawkandi Art   Karachi

SELECTED EXHIBITIONS
2005   Ifa Gallery Shared Existance (October 2005) Berlin
        NGMA- National Gallery of Modern Art
        Bombay
        Beyond Borders – Art of Pakistan
2004   Alhamra Old Masters · Young Voices Lahore
        High Point Centre of Printmaking , Minneapolis
        Minnesota, USA
        Pakistani Printmakers
        Rohtas Gallery Another Dawn Islamabad
        Ise Cultural Foundation Cover Girl: New York
        the Female Body and Islam in Contemporary Art

2003   43rd Premio Suzzara Suzzara, Itlay

2002   Harris Museum ArtSouthAsia England
2002   Artist's Residency at Gasworks Studios
        London
2002   11th Asian Art Biennale Dhaka
2001   Ivan Doughty Gallery, UNSW The Eye Still Seeks
        Sydney
2001   Vasl International Artists' Workshop, a Triangle
        Arts Trust Initiative Gadani
2001   White Columns Global Women Project   New
        York
2000   Another Vision Fifty years of painting and sculpture
        in Pakistan London
1998   Bluecoat Gallery Lines of Desire A touring
        exhibition   Liverpool Liverpool
1996   Rohtas Gallery Islamabad
1994   7th International Dhaka Biennale Dhaka
        Bradford Art Gallery An Intelligent Rebellion
        Bradford
        6th National Exhibition of Visual Arts Islamabad

AWARDS
2003   Prize, 43rd Premio Suzzara Itlay
2003   National Excellence Award, 8th National Exb.
        Visual Arts Pakistan
2002   Lever Brothers, 1st Lux Awards for Visual Artist of
        the year Pakistan

CURRENT
1991-   current Faculty Fine Art · Indus Valley School of Art
        and Architecture,   Karachi
2003-2004   Head of Painting Dept. · Indus Valley
        School of Art and Architecture
2000-   current Founder member and working group of the
        Vasl International Artists' Workshop, a Triangle
        Network initiative, UK

SHAMYL KHUHRO

FREELANCE PHOTOGRAPHER
from 1999 – continuing: Works featured in national/
international journals, newspapers and magazines
including, *The New York Times*, Discovery Channel, *Libas
International*, *Zameen*, *Visage*, *Mr.*, *Newsline*, *Herald*, *She*,
Women's Own, *Diva*, *Hamsafar*, *The News*, *Daily Times*, *Dawn*,
Jang, and *Fashion Collection*

FASHION:
Worked with several designers including Rizwan Beyg,
Sonya Batla, Sana Safinaz, Umar Sayeed, Samar Mehdi,
Deepak Perwani, Sanya Muneer, Nadya Shah, Maheen
Khan, Khaadi, Labels, Levis, Nike and Maria B.

PHOTO JOURNALISM:
Collaborated with journalists on assignments covering

Pakistani politics and society. Issues have included
the Afghan refugee crisis, madrassahs, Islamisation
in the Northern Areas, violence and drug consumption
amongst teenagers, night cricket in Ramadan and the o
restaurants of Karachi
Commercial/Product photography: Worked for several
Companies and NGO's including Standard Chartered
Bank, Glaxo Smith Kline, Novartis, KFC, AKD, Dawlance,
LG, Candyland, Bisconi, Supreme tea, Unilever, Shell,
Data Steel, Younis Textile, Mary Stopes, Ahung, Aga Kha
Educational Development and Sindh Education Foundati

GROUP EXHIBITIONS:
"Photography as Art" curated by Tapu Javeri, Arts Counc
        Karachi, June 2001
"Contemporary photojournalism from Pakistan" curated
        by Tehmina Ahmed, Alliance Francaise, Dhaka, 2
        November - 02 December, 2002
"Portraits" curated by Tapu Javeri, Arts Council, Karachi
        July 2003
"An idea of Perfection" curated by Aasim Akhtar and
        organised by Pakistan National Council of the Ar
        May 2002

AWARD NOMINEE:
For the Lux Style Awards in category of fashion
        photography · 2002, 2003 and 2005.

EDUCATION:
O-levels: Karachi Grammar School, Karachi, 1990
Bachelor of Arts: Karachi University, 1995

ADNAN LOTIA

EDUCATION
2005   Academy of Art University, San Francisco, CA
2003   Harvard University, Cambridge, MA
2001   B.Sc. Studio Art, New York University School of
        Education, New York, NY
1999   Vassar College, Poughkeepsie, NY

EXPERIENCE
2005   Designer, Oxford University Press, Karachi
2002   Full-time faculty, Indus Valley School of Art &
        Architecture, Karachi
2001   Senior Shows 2001, Rosenfield Gallery, New York,
        NY
2001   Artist assistant, Laura Parnes/Eric Heist, Brookly
        NY
2001   Intern, Momenta Art, Brooklyn, NY
2000   Sound & lighting, Hollywood Inferno, New York, N
2000   Portraiture, Rupert Goldsworthy Gallery, New York
        NY
2000   Intern, Luhring Augustine Gallery, New York, NY

RAH MAHBUB

EDUCATION:
. P.E.C.H.S College Karachi · 1987 – Fine Art |
Literature | Psychology

CHRONOLOGY:
97 – Presently teaching photography at the Indus
Valley School of Art and Architecture. I teach
the Communication & Design and the Fine
Arts Department basic to an advance level
(Photography Studio Minors). Furthermore
whenever time permits freelance work carries on in
the sidelines as before.
A recent list of clients includes: Khaddi Cloths line
· Pie in the Sky bakery · Morinaga Infant Cereal
· Arts and Gems Jewelers – Copper & Steel – Club
Havana
94 to 1996 freelance work for various publications
and commercial photography for national and
multinational companies. –The News – Dawn·
Women's Own – She – Visage – Fashion Collection
etc
93   Worked as an in-house photographer for
advertising agency R·Lintas
90 to 1993 Freelance photographic work for various local
publications.

ARTIST'S DETAILS:
ave been a professional photographer for more
an 17 years. Being self taught, I learnt mostly from
ooks, magazines and libraries found locally or obtained
ooks through friends and relatives from abroad.
ver these years as a professional I did fine art
hotography for personal self expression and freelance
hotography for various publications, national and
ultinational company's, kept this erratic pace for long,
ntil I joined Indus Valley School of Art and Architecture
1997 to teach photography. Presently freelance work
at its minimum and being a fulltime faculty member
various levels is at its maximum. And the petite spare
oments life gives me, are spent in plans to travel in
earch of fresh images, and to experiment further with
ew techniques and processes. Venturing into Digital Art
eemed natural after being involved with time-honored old
lternative Photography Processes.

PHILOSOPHY
hotography is a path, a sequence of events to be lived
nd experienced that helps you discover yourself and the
eople and places in your near and distant environments.
: is not a fixed state of mind or being but an evolving
nedium, to take the edge off the weight some of us can feel
n conveying our feelings, beliefs and desires. In short not
ll of us are verbal enough in putting into words any intense

visual rush witnessed.
As a visual artist we are most satisfied in expressing
ourselves when we photograph subjects that give us a
spiritual or an emotional rush. There is no traditional way
of perceiving the subject, only diverse ways in which it can
be experienced. What is essential is how the subject looks
and feels to you. In the eye of the beginner there are many
possibilities; in the eye of the specialist there are only a
few.

STYLE :
Architecture, Landscapes, and Environmental Portraits,
Traditional and Alternative Photography Processes in Color
and Black & White.

TECHNIQUE:
I work with medium format or 35mm cameras, analog
or digital. Photographs are usually produced on Fuji or
Kodak paper, and for the various alt-processes fine grain
watercolor paper. For the fine art work produced image
manipulation is at times applied using traditional darkroom
methods or digital techniques.

SOLO EXHIBITIONS
February 2000 – Hues Within
Sadequain Gallery –Frere Hall –Karachi
SG Forum Art Gallery (Alliance Francaise)·Karachi
December 1996 · Intention· Sadequain Gallery –Frere Hall·
Karachi
September 1993 · Rendezvous with France · Alliance
Francaise –Karachi
GROUP EXHIBITIONS
Photo Exhibition, Singular Medium: Multiple Frames
15th to 18th Jan 2005 at the Italian Cultural
Center – New Delhi ·India
Kodak Photo Vision 2004 – PSK Photographic Society of
Karachi
10th – 12th June at The Arts Council Of Karachi
– Pakistan
11th Asian Art Biennale, Osmani Memorial Hall · Dhaka,
Bangladesh from 15th January to 2nd February
2004.
Center for Contemporary Art in Sacramento U.S.A for the
show Digital Visions.·2002
Interrogating Diversity · February 1 · March 13, 2002
Betty Rymer Gallery · Chicago, Illinois United
States of America (312)443-3703
online exhibition · Break on Through to the Other
Side: Focus on Pakistan | A Cyber-Sent Art
Exhibition of Contemporary Art from Pakistan
February 2002 – An Idea of Perfection – (PNCA) the
Pakistan National Council of the Arts
Alhamra Gallery · Lahore · Pakistan
September 2001·Karavan Karachi ·Photography, Gallery
Sadequain, Karachi· Pakistan.

1994| 1995 |1996 |1997| PSK· Photographic Society of
Karachi
Ether Echoes –9th November 2005 – VM Gallery

ADNAN MALIK

EDUCATION
Vassar College, Poughkeepsie, NY December 2002
Bachelor's of Arts in Film Theory and Production with a
correlate in Public Economics Cumulative GPA 3.5
Recipient of Jane Dealy Wirsig Memorial Prize in
Recognition of Accomplishment and Promise in the
field of Journalism

MEDIA RELATED POSITIONS
Karachi International Film Festival, festival organizer/head
of television promotion
Charlotte Street Productions, Senior Researcher/
Production Assistant NY, NY July-Jan 2004
· Led the research team for Director Eugene Jarecki's ('Trial
of Henry Kissinger') feature length documentary
"Why We Fight" (Winner Grand Jury Prize,
Sundance 2005) on emergence of the U.S military-
industrial complex.
· Researched classified documents, the Internet and
primary sources to piece together arguments.
Researched various archive companies and served
as a liaison between the international al archive
houses (Al-Jazeera, Abu Dhabi tv etc.) and the
production company, as well as shot high profile
interviews on DVCam.
Miramax, Marketing and New Media Office Intern NY, New
York Summer 2002
· Researched and developed an online database of
marketable sites for Gangs Of New York etc, and
organized trailer checks, viewed and logged dailies,
and studied role of demographics in marketing.
InCite Pictures/ Cine Qua Non, Story developer/researcher
NY, New York Summer 2002
·Researched and developed PBS documentary on Muslim
and Jewish Youth basketball team in NY.
Ridley Scott America, Production Assistant and Office
Intern LA, California Summer 2001
·Assisted on commercial shoots, viewed director's reels,
logged tapes and contributed to the office
inventory.
Warren Cowan and Associates, Publicity Intern, LA,
California Summer 2001
·Served as a personal assistant to a-list celebrity clients,
coordinated their schedules, represented PR firm
on photo shoots, created press kits, assisted in
general office work.
SKG DreamWorks, Personal Assistant, Poughkeepsie, New
York April 2001

·Worked as a PA on the set of "Time Machine".

PRODUCTION AND OTHER RELATED EXPERIENCE

Director of graphics, montages, red carpet and behind the scenes for the Lux Style Awards, 2005.

Director, Cinematographer, Editor for "Social Circus", a behind the scenes documentary on the making of a music video in the red light district, Lahore.

Director, researcher, Writer and Cinematographer of "The Forgotten Song", a feature length documentary on the demise of cinema culture in Pakistan.

Directed and wrote "Bijli", a documentary on a drag queen in Manhattan, NY. (Winner: Best Short at the KARA film festival 2003, Best Short at the Delhi Digital film festival 2004 and Regional Finalist at the Student Academy Awards, 2003 USA etc.). The film was also bought by New York University where I served as a regular guest lecturer.

Pakistani trainer/teacher for British council workshop on filmmaking in Pakistan. (Jan-March 2005) as well as a regular lecturer at Arena Multi-Media Colleges in Karachi.

Director of multi-media project on Afghani immigrants, "Deconstructing the Terrorist".

Cinematographer on 16mm documentary on "Gogol Bordello" a Ukrainian folk-rock band (Screened at Student Academy Awards 2002, The Whitney Museum, KARA, Austin film festivals etc.)

Director/Cinematographer for Pakistani sequence in acclaimed documentary "In the Name of Allah"

Organizing Committee member for 4th and 5th KARA film festival.

Judge for Unilever's annual All-Pakistan art competition.

Cinematographer for Marly Hornik's music video 'Just a Girl', played at music channels in the US.

Researcher/PA for VH-1 production of 'Driven' featuring Paula Abdul

Researcher, Designer, Marketer for satirical t-shirt company entitled "Urban Turban".

AFSHAR MALIK

SOLO AND TWO PERSON SHOWS

2004   Solo Show of paintings at Canvas Art Gallery Karachi

2003   A two-person show of drawings with Anwar Saeed at Canvas Karachi

2000   Solo show of paintings and mix media prints at Chawkandi Art Gallery, Karachi

1995   A two-person show of Lithographs, etchings with Anwar Saeed at Chawkandi Art Gallery, Karachi

1993   Solo show "42 Etching Prints" at The Art Gallery, Islamabad

1990   Solo show 'Slade Portfolio' · Lithographs and

Etchings at Rohtas Gallery, Islamabad

1989   Solo show 'Slade Portfolio' · Lithographs and Prints at Zamana Interior, Lahore

GROUP SHOWS

2004   "Contemporary printmakers from Pakistan" a group show at Highpoint, Minneapolis USA and Appalechian University North Carolina USA

2004   Group show at "Khaas" art gallery Islamabad.

2003   Vasl workshop's exhibition held at VM Gallery Karachi

2000   A three person show of paintings at Sim Sim Gallery, Lahore

2000   A group show of drawings at Sim Sim Gallery, Lahore,

2000   Contemporary Art from Pakistan in Tehran, Iran

1999   A three-person show of paintings and ceramics at Sim Sim Gallery, Lahore

1997   "Printmakers from Pakistan" a group show held at Bradford Art Museum, Bradford UK

1996   Group show of paintings, Colombo Sri Lanka

1995   A three-person show of etchings "Etched Images" at the NCA Gallery, Lahore

1994   'Scope' · group shows by the faculty of National College of Arts at NCA Gallery, 1999   Lahore

1994   A group show of Sculptures at the NCA Gallery, Lahore

1993   A group show 'Printmakers from NCA' · etchings and lithographs at the American Center Gallery Lahore

1988   Post graduate show at Slade School of Fine Arts, London UK

TEACHING EXPERIENCE

1983 · to date National College of Arts Lahore
Teaching drawing, painting and printmaking

OTHER PROFESSIONAL EXPERIENCES

1978 · 1979 'The Muslim' Islamabad
Staff Cartoonist for a daily English newspaper

1979 · 1980 'DHANNAK' Lahore
Staff Cartoonist and illustrator for a monthly society magazine

1979 · 1980 'JANG' Lahore
Cartoonist for a daily urdu newspaper

1989 · 2001 'The Friday Times' Lahore
Cartoonist for a weekly magazine · newspaper

1985 · 1986 'MIDAS' Lahore
Worked as an illustrator and visualizer in an advertising agency

1978 · 1994 'Design & Illustration' Lahore
Worked as a free lance designer and illustrator for ten children's story books and posters for AGHS · an NGO

1978 · 1994 'Pakistan Television' Lahore

Worked as a freelance illustrator for children programs

AMBIANCE INSTALLATIONS

1997 · 2000 Lahore
Designed and installed ambiance of Basant fes... · a dinner hosted by *The News* for their clients a social elite:
At the Mughal's "Kamran's Baradari" · an islan... River Ravi
At "Evernew Studios" a film studio
At the Mughal's "Asif Jah's Haveli"
For Pakistan Cricket Board to award the cricket stars at "Escort Gardens"

QUALIFICATIONS

Graduation in Fine Arts
1974 – 1978 Diploma in Fine Arts National College of A... Lahore
Higher Diploma in Fine Arts
1986 · 1988 Slade School of Arts University College London, UK

PERSONAL

9th March 1955 Bahawalpur, Pakistan

SEEMA NUSRAT

ACADEMIC QUALIFICATION

Specialization in miniature painting, Indus valley schoo... art and architecture, Karachi, 2003

Bachelor of fine art, Indus valley school of art and architecture, Karachi, 2002

HSC, Sindh Board of Intermediate Education, home economics College for Women, Karachi, 1998

SSC, Sindh Board of Secondary Education, little folk's School, Karachi, 1996

ART EXHIBITIONS

Miniature painting Thesis show, Indus valley school of a... and architecture, 2003

Group show, "Women painters of Pakistan", organized b... the Pakistan national council of the arts, Karac... January 2003

Group Exhibition, "Emerging Talents", VM Art Gallery, February, 2003

Thesis Degree Show, Indus Valley School of Art and Architecture, 2002

Kara-sculpture exhibition at the Alliance Française de Karachi, 2002

Group Show of works by students from various art institutions at Frere Hall, 2001

Group show/Painting competition, "environmental disaster", Frere hall, 2000.

stant teacher, miniature painting department,
january2003
tume design for SAF games (Islamabad). 2003
ducted arts and craft work shop, Indus valley school of
art and architecture, Karachi,2000

HID RAZA

7   Born in Delhi
0   Diploma in Fine Arts, Central Institute of Arts and
     Crafts
0   Graduated Karachi University

O SHOWS ABROAD
8   Castle Zeilitzheim, Pak-German Cultural Exchange
     Programme, Germany
8   Geo Gallery, Berlin, Germany
9   Anna Blum-Haus, Heideberg, Germany
1   Atellier Galleries, Reillingen, Germany
5   Museum of Modern Art, Amman, Jordan
8   International Visitor's Programme, Fellowship and
     Residency Programme at SUNY New Paltz, New
     York, USA
9   Asian Society, River Oak Bank, Houston, Texas,
     USA
2   Amnesty International Osterrcity, Bezirk Museum,
     Vienna

O SHOWS IN PAKISTAN
0   Goethe Institut, Karachi
3   Arts Council, Karachi
5   Contemporary Art Gallery, Rawalpindi
8   Indus Gallery, Karachi
1   Arts Council, Karachi
3   Indus Gallery, Karachi
5   Selectif, Karachi
6   Chawkandi Art, Karachi
7   Chawkandi Art, Karachi
8   Rohtas Gallery, Rawalpindi
9   Danish Art Gallery, Karachi
0   Interior Art Gallery, Islamabad
0   Indus Art Gallery, Karachi

UP SHOWS IN PAKISTAN
1   Indus Gallery, Karachi
0   Fourteen Women Painters, Indus Gallery, Karachi
1   National Exhibition, PNCA, Islamabad
4   Arts Council, Karachi
4   Indus Gallery, Karachi
8   National Biennale, Karachi
0   Ziggurat Gallery, Karachi
2   Chawkandi Art, Karachi

1993   Indus Gallery, Karachi
1994   Indus Gallery, Karachi
1995   Pakistan American Cultural Center, Karachi
1996   Indus Gallery, Karachi
1997   Chawkandi Art, Karachi
1998   Ziggurat Gallery, Karachi
1999   Alhamra Gallery, Lahore
2000   Croweater Gallery, Lahore
2002   The Art Gallery, Karachi
2003   National Art Exhibition at Alhamra Gallery, Lahore
2004   Arts Council, Karachi
2005   Ejaz Gallery, Lahore

COLLECTIONS
Citibank, Deutsche Bank, Standard Chartered Bank,
     National Council of Arts & Bradford Museum,
     England.
1994   Established Studio Art, an academy of fine arts
     and graphics
2003   Principal of Central Institute of Arts and Crafts,
     Arts Council, Karachi

SAEED RAHMAN

GROUP EXHIBITIONS
2004   Melange, Canvas Gallery, Karachi, Pakistan
2004   Fatal Love: South Asian American Art Now, Queens
     Musuem of Art, New York, USA

SCREENINGS
2003   Haseena 420, Cinema Classics, New York, USA
2004   Haseena 420, South Asian Seattle Film Festival,
     Seattle, WA

MUGHEES RIAZ

EDUCATION:
1999   MFA (Painting), Dept. of Fine Arts, University of
     Punjab, Lahore
1997   BFA (Painting), Dept. of Fine Arts, University of
     Punjab, Lahore

SOLO EXHIBITIONS:
2005   Khas, The Art Gallery, Islamabad
2004   Canvas Gallery, Karachi
2001   Ejaz Art Gallery, Lahore

GROUP EXHIBITIONS:
2005   V.M Art Gallery, Karachi
2004   Kunj Art Gallery, Karachi
2004   Image Of Pakistan?, World Bank, Islamabad
2003   Canvas Gallery, Karachi
2003   Ejaz Gallery, Lahore

2003   Mok Wod Hoe Art Association, Spirit of Asia, Korea
2003   The Vision of landscape?, Pakistan National Council
     of Arts, Islamabad
2003   8th National Exhibition, Alhmara Art Gallery,
     Lahore
2002   Tariq Jay Art Gallery, Karachi
2001   Takhti Exhibition, Frere Hall, Karachi
2000   Millenium Show, Ejaz Gallery, Lahore
1999   Alhamra Art Gallery, Lahore
1999   Anna Molka Art Gallery, Lahore

Also participated in all exhibitions held by the Punjab
Artists Association and the Young Artist's Association,
since 1994.

EXPERIENCE AND AWARDS:
Visiting Lecturer, Painting, University of Punjab, Lahore,
     since 1999
MFA First Class
1st Prize in Painting, Directorate General of Society
     Welfare, Women Dept., Govt. of Punjab, Lahore,
     2001
National Excellence Award (Visual Arts), 2003

LALA RUKH

EDUCATION:
Master of Fine Arts (MFA) from the University of Chicago,
     Chicago, USA, 1976.
Master of Fine Arts (MFA) from the University of the Punjab,
     Lahore, 1970.

PROFESSION:
Artist, educationist

AREAS OF EXPERTISE:
Teaching; photography; conceptualizing courses for
informal art education and skill development for grassroots
activists, organizing and conducting the same; Design and
production of posters, pamphlets, booklets and manuals
for women activists.

EXPERIENCE:
2000:   Director, MA(Hons.) Visual Art, Dept. of Fine Art,
     NCA
1998:   Associate Professor, National College of Art,
     Lahore.
1982 – 1998: Assistant Professor, National College of Arts,
     Lahore.
1978 – 1982: Lecturer: University of the Punjab, Deptt. of
     Fine Arts, Lahore.
1971 – 1974: Art Teacher: Lahore American School.
1977 – 1980: Conducted Art and Photography Classes: Art
     Centre, Lahore.

1981: Member, National Committee for the Preparation of Curriculum for Arts & Crafts Teacher Training Course

Feb. 20001. Awarded' The Best Teacher Award 2000'. By the University Grants Commission. Islamabad.

EXHIBITIONS:

Aug 2005. One 2 One. 58 years. 58 Artists. Alhamra Art Gallery. Lahore

Feb. 2005. Beyond Borders. Art from Pakistan. National Gallery of Modern Art. Mumbai, India.

Nov. 2004. Art from Pakistan. House of Commons. London. UK.

July 2004. Exhibition of Works: 1980-2004. VM Art Gallery. ZVMG Rangoonwala Centre. Karachi.

April 2004. Exhibition of Works: 1980-2003. Zahoor-ul Akhlaque Gallery. National College of Arts. Lahore.

Dec. 2003. Group show at Nairang Gallery. Lahore

April 2002. National Art Exhibition. , Artist's Association of Pakistan. Alhamra Art Gallery. Lahore.

March 2002. Let Peace Prevail. Exhibition of Women Artists. V.M. Gallery, Rangoonwala Centre. Karachi.

Jan 2001. Vasl International Artists' Workshop, at Gadani, Baluchistan. Organised and participated in the workshop and Exhibitions: Open day at Gadani, Balochistan. Exhibition: Gulgee Museum, Karachi. Pakistan

April 2000. Pakistan: Another Vision. Brunei Gallery, SOAS, London, UK June-Aug: Huddersfield Art Gallery.

Aug-Sept. Oldham Art Gallery

Sept-Nov. Victoria Art Gallery/Hotbath Gallery, Bath.

April 2000. Beginning and End of an Era. Ejaz Galleries. Lahore.

March 2000. Millennium Exhibition. Artist Association of Pakistan, Alhamra Art Gallery

Nov 99: 9th Asian Art Biennale Bangladesh,99. Bangladesh

May 99. Scope VII. Galerie NCA, Lahore

1997- 98. Women's Action Forum visualiser and coordinator of the commemorative project, to be installed at the Bagh-e-Jinnah, Lahore, Pakistan

Nov 97. "Open Wounds". Eicher Gallery. Delhi. India. (With Samina Mansuri).

Jan. 97. On the internet: "The Book of Lies". A mobile museum of Actual Art. http://www. floatingmuseum.com

Oct 96. The Book of Lies: Steirischer Herbst Festival. Graz. Austria

Aug 96. National Exhibition of Paintings. Pakistan Golden Jubilee Celebration. Alhambra, Lahore.

Jan 96. Exhibition of Pakistani Painters. 7th SAARC Festival, Pragati Maidan, New Delhi, India.

Oct 95. Exhibition of Pakistani Painters. Pakistan Festival (organised by Export Promotion Bureau) Birmingham Cultural Complex, Birmingham, England.

Aug 95. Exhibition of Women Painters. Conference of Muslim Women Parliamentarians. Islamabad.

Jan 95. "An Intelligent Rebellion" Women Artists of Pakistan, UNESCO headquarters, Paris, France.

1995: "An Intelligent Rebellion" Leicester city Art Gallery. England.

April 95. "Scope VI." Gallery NCA. National College of Arts, Lahore.

1994/95 "The Book of Lies," a mobile museum of International Artists, Los Angeles, USA

Oct 94. "An Intelligent Rebellion, Women Artists of Pakistan". Cartwright Hall,.Bradford. UK

April 94. Exhibition of 7 artists on the theme of violence organized by Goethe Institute, Karachi.

Feb 94. 'A Selection of Contemporary Paintings from Pakistan." Pacific Asia Museum. Pasadena, California, USA.

Feb 94. National Exhibition. Pakistan National Council of the Arts, Islamabad.

Feb 93. "Scope V" Gallery NCA, National College of Arts, Lahore.

March 93 "Printmakers from NCA". American Centre, Lahore.

April 93. Participated in an Artist's Camp and Exhibition on the theme of violence organized by the Goethe Institute, Lahore.

July 81. One Person Show of drawings, Galerie Hildebrand, Klagenfurt, Austria.

1980. One Person Show of drawings, PACC Gallery, Karachi.

1978. One Person Show of photographs - Maison de la Culture, Rennes, France.

1976. Two Persons Show of paintings and drawings at University of Chicago, Chicago, USA.

1970 to date: Numerous group shows in Pakistan; at Alhambra Art Centre, Lahore, National Exhibitions, Lahore Art Gallery, NCA gallery.

ANWAR SAEED

EDUCATION

1978 Bachelors in Fine Arts, National College of Arts, Lahore

1985 Post Graduate Studies (Printmaking/Book Illustration), Royal College of Arts, London

SELECTED EXHIBITIONS

2001 Vasl Artists Show, Amin Gulgee Gallery, Karachi

2000 Canvas Gallery, Karachi

2000 Pakistan Another Vision, UK

1999 Bata Pata, Harare, Mutare and Bulawayo, Zimbabwe

1999 The Art Gallery, Islamabad

1998 Chawkandi Art, Karachi

1997 Printmakers of Pakistan 1947-97, Bradford, UK

1996 EPB Painting Show, New Delhi, India

1996 Etchings, Chawkandi Art, Karachi

1995 The Art Gallery, Islamabad

1995 Paintings and Prints, Amman, Jordan

1995 Etched Images, Zahoorul Akhlaq Gallery, National College of Arts, Lahore

1994 Fifth International Biennale, Cairo, Egypt

1994 Seventh Asian Art Biennale, Dhaka, Bangladesh

1993 Contemporary painting in Pakistan, Pacific Asia Museum, California, USA

1992 Chawkandi Art, Karachi

1992 Nairang Gallery, Lahore

1992 Crossing Black Waters, City Gallery, Leicester, U

1990 Departures, Indesign, Lahore

1989 Art Now, Nairang Gallery, Lahore

1988 Chawkandi Art, Karachi

1987 Seven Artists from Pakistan, Oslo, Norway

1986 Chawkandi Art, Karachi

1986 Walls and Doors, Rohtas Gallery, Islamabad

1984 Windows, Rohtas Gallery, Islamabad

SHAKIL SAIGOL

Born in Calcutta in 1944, Saigol is a scion of a family of pioneering industrialists, who migrated to Pakistan when the partition of India took place. He was educated at St. Mary's, a missionary-run boys school in Rawalpindi and subsequently at Government College, Lahore where he defiantly took up Fine Arts and acquitted himself with distinction. He read history at The Queen's College, Oxford and returned to marry and to manage a family-owned textile mill in Rawalpindi. He unveiled his work for the first time at a one-man show in Lahore in 1991, a most reluctant debutant, yet at age 47 a senior artist, and according to some critics, the best-kept secret of the art world.

His life, according to him, was "fragmented" until he suffered a heart attack at age 42, which has had a profound impact on his life. Significantly, he perceives it as a re-birth, since the intimations of mortality have helped him to break away systematically from all those conditions and compromises which have hindered his creative growth and impulses. Today he successfully combines the designing and manufacturer of fine jewels and parenting with his wife, and paints "as much as he feels like"—often enough, in fact, to have a second one-man show in Karachi in October 1995.

His third solo exhibition at the Air Gallery, London in October 1999 was a huge success which, to an artist who remains unusually reticent about his work, was "intimidating". His private commissions of Jamavar shawls

tings have prevented him from having enough paintings
xhibit his deeply moving body of work on Afghanistan—
Land God Forgot. The SurSundari paintings proved to
 cathartic release from the pathos and morbidity of the
hanistan paintings.

kil Saigol's Paintings are represented in various
ibitions and collections in Pakistan and abroad. He lives
 works in Karachi, Pakistan.

ne: Muhammad Shakil Saigol
e of birth: 11-02-1944, Calcutta

UCATION
52   Senior Cambridge St. Mary's High School
       Rawalpindi, Pakistan.
56   B.A. Govt. College Lahore, Pakistan.
58   B.A. The Queen's College Oxford, England.

LO EXHIBITIONS
vate World Lahore Art Gallery Lahore 1991
ms Chawkandi Art Gallery Karachi   1995
r□sh Air Gallery London 1999
rSundari   Canvas Gallery Karachi 2004

ROUP EXHIBITIONS
 National Exhibition of Visual Arts PNCA Islamabad
       1996
awkandi Art Gallery Karachi 1999
ennale Sharjah Museum Sharjah 2001
aan Exhibition Gulgee Museum Karachi 2002
hawkandi Art Gallery Karachi 2002
's Gallery Karachi 2002
ational Art Exhibition Lahore 2003
l's Gallery Karachi 2003
ational Gallery of Modern Art Mumbai 2005
armony Show Mumbai 2005

RT CAMPS
rand Hyat Mumbai 2004
oenka Art Camp Madh Island 2005

ABAR SHEIKH

DUCATION
achelors of Design, Major Communication Design Indus
       Valley School of Art and Architecture, Karachi
       1999. Distinction in Thesis.
Sc, Pre Medical, DHA Degree College for Men, Karachi,
       1995, B-Grade
Matric, Science Group, The City School, Karachi, 1993,
       A-Grade

VORK EXPERIENCE

Writer & Director for Diagram. Film Company initiated in
       Dec 00.
Faculty.   Team for final year thesis at the Indus Valley
       School of Art & Architecture Karachi.
Faculty (part time) University of Karachi, Visual Studies
       Department.
Faculty (part time) Textile Institute of Pakistan Karachi.
Faculty (part time). Discovery Center, Informatics Karachi.
       Head of A/V Department Karachi.
Pyramid Productions, Director, Nov 00 to Current, Films
       and Commercials.
Pyramid Productions, Assistant Director, July 00 to Nov
       00. Projects: Dalda Ka Dastarkhwan, Benson and
       Hedges Global Beat & Various other Weekend
       World Programs.
Asiatic JWT, Associate Art Director, Jan 00 to Jun 00.
       Clients: Close up, Sunsilk, Kodak, Gulf Commercial
       Bank, Trakker, Lux.
Asiatic Advertising, Summer Internship, 1999. Projects:
       Singer, Lipton, Kodak.
(Option 2), Art Director, 1998-1999. Projects: ACE AIMS,
       Franklin Rolodex, Philips Whirlpool.

MAJOR PROJECTS WITH DIAGRAM
Currently writing and directing commercials, for local &
       international brands, e.g.; McDonalds, Unilever,
       Nestle, Coca-Cola, Tapal Tea, Dawn bread, Olivia
       cosmetics Etc...
Experimental short film 'Tabdeeli'. Completed and
       premiered Jan 2005.
Corporate documentaries for Multinational companies e.g.;
       Shell Pakistan, ABN AMRO Bank.
Line production and research for 'Must Qalander', a
       German short film project from HFF Berlin.
'The color of Red'- Experimental short film currently under
       pre production. (Dresden – Germany)
Conceptualized, choreographed and directed music videos
       for Strings, Jal, Ali Haider, Mizraab, Mauj, Sajjad
       Ali, Haroon ki Awaz, Kara van, Faakhir and Others.
       00 to present.
Written, directed & produced short Films - "Belief", "The
       Golden Flight".
Tapal Tea: Branded Music Video for song titled Dewayne
       2002.
Conceptualized and Produced TV commercials for Lever
       Brothers Pakistan Ltd.
Askari Commercial Bank, Television Commercial.
Coca Cola Music Masti. Produced and directed six episodes
       of this music / travel show.
Freelance Direction for launch of Pakistan's first
       independent TV Channel – Indus Vision.

PARTICIPATIONS
The Red Projekt (Germany):
At present working, on 'Cityuations', a joint experimental

film project featuring artists / filmmakers from
       Poland and Germany.
Kinobuss (Estonia):
Participation with this unique traveling project, throughout
       the Estonian country side, spreading awareness for
       motion picture, on both animated and live action
       formats.
17.0 Film-fest Dresden & 03 Exchange Forum 'Perspectives'
       2005:
Participation at the sixteenth international film festival
       Dresden presented and premiered Tabdeeli for
       European audiences.
16.0 Film-fest Dresden & 03 Exchange Forum
       'Perspectives' 2004
Participation at the sixteenth international film festival
       Dresden & continuation of film / animation project
       between self & European filmmakers, April 2004.
       Dresden – Tallinn. The project initiated, is currently
       in its developmental and funding stages.
Cultural Grant/Scholarship Germany 2003:
Selected and invited by the Cultural foundation of
       Saxony, to spend a month through Germany, with
       opportunities to meet and interact with German
       filmmakers, institutes, and potential partners.
15.0 Film-fest Dresden & 02 Exchange Forum
       'Perspectives' 2003:
Participation at the fifteenth international film festival
       Dresden & initialization of film/ animation project
       between self & European filmmakers, April 2003.
       Dresden – Krakow.
14.0 Film-fest Dresden Germany 2002:
Participation at the fourteenth film festival Dresden & the
       exchange forum "Perspectives on Animation Films"
       with European filmmakers, March/April 2002.
       Dresden – Prague.

DUSK, EXPERIMENTAL AMBIENT MUSIC:
Project started in 1994.
Direction and performance of sound scopes in studio, 1995
       through 1999
CD (M. I. N. A) Launched internationally by Hibernia
       Productions 1999, Portugal
CD (Hearts Of darkness) launched locally by Dusk Horde
       productions 2002, Karachi – Pakistan
CD (Jahilia) launched internationally through Epidemie
       records (Czech Republic) 2003.
Jahilia Autumn tour 2004 – tour with the project through
       out Czech Republic

EXPERIMENTAL FILM:
Workshop in experimental film making at Goethe Institut,
       1999.
Working with group of visual and performing artists to
       create multidimensional performance based
       activities:

Giving workshops at various educational institutions, helping spread film, music and other art forms.
Produced and recorded tracks with 'Aufgang'. Experimental sound design project.
Improvising of music, performance and visual arts at PACC, 1999.
Theater workshops and performances with Katha, Dramasala and Unplugged, 1996 through 1999.
Short appearance in TV play "Pindar", 1999.
Photography and visualization for Mizraab, and Dramasala, 1998-1999.

GANDA BANDA AND THE 3-D CATS:
Art oriented world music band formed in 1997.
Credits as bass player and vocalist.
Major concerts through 1997-2002.

SHAKEEL SIDDIQUI

EDUCATION
1970–72 Short courses at Art Students league of New York, USA
1975 Diploma in Fine Art Painting, Central Institute of Arts and Crafts, Karachi

SELECTED EXHIBITIONS
2001 Beyond the Surface, Highgate Gallery, London, UK
2001 Takhti Exhibition, Galerie Sadequain, Karachi
2000 Chawkandi Art, Karachi
1996 Indus Gallery, Karachi
1992 Second International Art Biennale, Sharjah, UAE
1988 First International Art Biennale, Alhamra Art Center, Lahore
1987, 84 Sindh Artists Exhibiton, Karachi
1978 Atelier BM, Karachi
1976 National Exhibition, Lahore
1975 National Exhibition, Karachi
1972 Maine Community Center, Portland, USA

AWARDS AND HONOURS
1999 Invited by Medecin Sans Frontiers to participate in the world's longest painting
1988 Best Entry (oils), First International Art Biennale, Lahore
1987 Dadabhoy Gold Medal, Sindh Artists Exhibition, Karachi
1985, 84 Best Entry (oils), Sindh Artists Exhibition, Karachi

TASADUQ SOHAIL

D.O.B – 30th October, 1930, Jallender, India

EDUCATION

Studied art at St.Martin's College of Art, London, UK

EXHIBITIONS
2005 Khaas Art Gallery, Islamabad
2004 Zenaini Art Gallery, Karachi
2003 Croweaters Gallery, Lahore
2003 Canvas Art Gallery, Karachi
2001 Indus Gallery, Karachi
2000 Indus Gallery, Karachi
1999 Indus Gallery, Karachi
1998 Indus Gallery, Karachi
1998 Nomad Centre and Art Gallery, Islamabad
1997 Lahore Art Gallery, Lahore
1997 Hotel Intercontinental, Dubai
1997 Indus gallery, Karachi
1996 Indus Gallery, Karachi
1995 Mermaid Gallery, London
1994 Indus Gallery, Karachi
1993 Boundary gallery, London
1993 Cachet Art Marstrich, Holland
1993 Indus gallery, Karachi
1993 Art Heritage, New Delhi
1992 Gallery 2000, Sweden
1991 South Bank Centre, London
1991 Lahore Art Gallery, Lahore
1991 Indus Gallery, Karachi
1990 Westbourne Gallery, London
1989 Nairang Galleries, Lahore
1989 Indus Gallery, Karachi
1988 Playhouse, Nottingham
1987 Horizon Gallery, London
1986 Rohtas, Rawalpindi
1986 Alhamra, Lahore
1986 Indus Gallery, Karachi
1985 Indus Gallery, Karachi
1979 October Gallery, London
1977 Indus Gallery, Karachi
1976 Heathordon Gallery, London

PRIVATE COLLECTIONS
British Arts Council, London and Victoria and Albert Museum, London

DOCUMENTARIES
On BBC, UK in 1979 and Channel 4, UK in 1987

RADIO INTERVIEWS
BBC London, BBC for India, BBC for Pakistan, Radio Nottingham and Voice of America.

ADEELA SULEMAN

Born on December 9th 1970 in Karachi, Pakistan.

EDUCATION:
BFA in Sculpture 1999, with Distinction, Indus Valley School of Art and Architecture, Karachi, Pakistan
MA in International Relations 1995, University of Karachi Karachi, Pakistan.

SELECTED GROUP EXHIBITIONS:
2005 Urban /Culture, cp Biennale 2005, Jakarta, Indonesia.
2005 Beyond Borders, National Gallery of Modern Art, Bombay, India.
2004 Caravan Café, Art from central Asia, Enrico Mascelloni. P.129.
2004 Spielen mit geladenem Gewehr (Playing with the loaded gun), Kunsthalle Fridericianum Kassel, Germany.
2003 24 Frames per Second, Kara Film Fest, Karachi, Pakistan.
2003 43rd Premio Suzzara, Associazione Galleria Del Premio Suzzara, Italy.
2003 Playing with the loaded Gun, Apex Art, New York, U.S.A.
2003 Group Show, Canvas Gallery, Karachi, Pakistan.
2002 Imagined Workshop-2nd Fukuoka Asian Art Triennale, Fukuoka, Japan.
2001 The Thakhti Show, Freer Hall, Karachi, Pakistan.

SELECTED CATALOGUES AND REVIEWS:
2005 Urban/Culture, cp biennale 2005,Jakarta, Indonesia. P.212,213
2005 Exploring Artistic Tradition, Quddus Mirza.Dawn Gallery,March 26th 2005.
2005 Beyond Borders, Art from Pakistan.Curated by Quddus Mirza,Dr Surya Doshi.
2004 Art in the time of Globalization, Amara Ali. Art India, The art News Magazine of India.vol ix issue iv.p 58.
2004 Women artist and Institution-Builders are Agents of Positive Change.interview with Salima Hashmi by Atteqa Ali. Art India, The Art News Magazine of India.vol ix issue iv.p 72.
2004 Different Kind of Voilence, Atteqa Ali. Art India, The Art News Magazine of India.vol ix issue iv.p 75.
2004 43rd Premio Suzzara. Curated by Martina Corgnati, Nicola Marras, Enrico Mascelloni. p. 66,67,88
2002 Unveiling the Visible- Lives and Works of Women Artist of Pakistan, Salima Hashmi. p.183-184
2002 Imagined Workshop- 2nd Fukuoka Asian Art Triennale.p12, 13, 122.
2002 Documents of Art Exchange Program-2nd Fukuoka Asian Art Triennale.p.13
2002 Chali ban than kay Dulhania.Herald.2002
2002 Feminity for Fukuoka, Quddus Mirza, Encore, The News march 17th 2002.

Fabricating Femininity, Art India Magazine. The Art
News Magazine of India. vol vii issue i. p 82, 84.
The Takhti Exhibition.Curated by Sheherzade Alam.
P.10
Urban Voices IV. P.22,23
Art of The 'New',Muna Siddiqui.Encore,The News
Dec.19th 1999.

AR TAHIR

thar Tahir was the 1974 Rhodes Scholar for Pakistan
iel College, Oxford, where he read English Language
Literature. Before his Masters at Oxford University, he
editor of The Ravi, the literary journal of Government
ege, Lahore. In 1979 he was the Rotary International
olar at the University of Pennsylvania and read
parative Religions and Muslim Architecture. He
awarded the Hubert H. Humphrey Fellowship to the
ersity of Southern California in 1984.

critical and creative work and translations from Urdu
Punjabi have been published in Pakistan and abroad.
has edited five occasional volumes of Pakistan English
try, published a collection of short stories, of essays
three volumes of poems: the latest *Yielding Years*
01) was awarded the top national prize for Literature
nglish—the Patras Bokhari Award—by the Pakistan
demy of Letters. His poems have been set as text
econdary schools and 'O' level courses, included in
eral Oxford University Press (OUP) anthologies and also
slated into Urdu and Chinese. His fourth volume of
try *Body-Loom* is due from OUP.

pioneering work on a nineteenth century Punjabi poet,
dir Yar: A Critical Introduction (1988), won the Shah Abdul
if Bhitai Award 1990 and the National Book Council
ze, 1991. He collaborated with Prof. Christopher Shackle
the School for Oriental and African Studies, London on
shim's *Sassi* (1986).

books on art and calligraphy include *Calligraphy &*
lligraph-art (UNESCO, 2002), *Pakistan Colors* (OUP,
01), *Bestower's Court* (PCG, 1999), *Khalid Iqbal: A*
rtfolio (1997), and *Lahore Colors* (1997), which won the
ze for the best book, the Allama Iqbal Award, 1998.

stower's Court, on the monumental calligraphy and
lligraph-art rendered by the Pakistan Calligraph-artists
uild in the mosque-shrine complex of the eleventh century
tron saint of Lahore, Ali Hujveri, won the Allama Iqbal
vard 2000.

founded the Pakistan Calligraph-artists Guild (PCG) in
97. He has curated four International exhibitions (1998,

1999, 2000, 2004), one national exhibition (2000) and
two two-nation exhibitions (2003, 2005) of calligraphy and
calligraph-art. He has lectured on culture and penmanship
at home and abroad including at the Cartwright Hall
Museum, Bradford, Cambridge University (U.K), the 11th
Holy Quran International Conference Tehran, Iran etc.

He has participated in several international and national
shows. His calligraph-art work figures in public and private
collections including that of the Pakistan Foreign office, Ali
Hujveri's mosque-shrine complex, Lahore (21' x 5' mural
in the Samac Hall) etc. He has designed the logos of the
Chenab College, Jhang and PCG. He has designed book
jackets and covers for literary journals and magazines.

Athar Tahir was awarded the Tamgha-i-Imtiaz/Medal of
Distinction for Literature in the Independence Day Honours
List.